LIST
of
EMIGRANTS *to* AMERICA
from
LIVERPOOL
1697-1707

Transcribed by

Elizabeth French

Originally published: *The New England Historical and Genealogical Register,* Vols. LXIV and LXV
Reprinted: New England Historic Genealogical Society, Boston, 1913
Reprinted: Genealogical Publishing Co., Inc.
Baltimore, 1962, 1969, 1978, 1983, 2010
Library of Congress Catalogue Card Number 63-754
ISBN 978-0-8063-0153-2
Made in the United States of America

LIST OF EMIGRANTS TO AMERICA FROM LIVERPOOL
1697-1707[1]

If I find Jno Lealand bound to Virg or Maryland I must write to his father a Tapeweaver in Salford.

Richard Hilton Apprentice to m^r Bryan Blundell for 11 yeares to Comen[ce] from his first Arrivall in Virginea Or Maryland, Indenture dated 28 of October 1697.

Martin Heyes, Apprentice to Thomas Johnson j^r Esqr (or Assignes) for 4 Yeares to Comence from his first arrivall in Virginea Or Maryland Indent[ure] dated ye 27 day of October 1697.

William Mosson Apprentice to Lewis Jenkins for 5 Yeares to Comence from his first Arrivall in Virginea Or Maryland Indenture dated the 29 day of October 1697

Isabell Conley Apprentice to Lewis Jenkins for 7 Years to Comence from hir first Arrivall at Virginea Or Maryland Indenture dated y^e : 23 day of October 1697

Margery Blundell to Henry Farar for 4 Years to Virginea [or] Maryland Indenture dated ye 11 : day of Novb^r 1697.

Law : GillGrist to Henry Farrar for 7 Years to Virginea [or] Maryland Indenture dated ye 11 day of Novr 1697

Tho : Sylvester to Henry Farrar for 7 Years to Virginea Or Maryland Indenture dated ye 11 day of Novr 1697

Isabel Conley to Lewis Jenkins for 7 Years to Virginea Or Maryland Indenture date ye 23 day of Novr 1697.

J^{no} Leek to m' Lewis Jenkins for 5 Years to Virginea Or Maryland Indenture dated ye first day of December 1697

Wm Ludloe [?] of Bradfrd in Yorkeshire App^r to m^r Wm Chantrell for 5 years to Virgin^a or Maryland

Wm Gibson to Randle Galloway for 4 Years to Virginea or Maryland Indenture dated ye first day of December 1697 —

J^{no} Webster to Randle Galloway for 8 Years to Virginea or Maryland

[ ]	Green (p^r m^r Parrs order) to Wm Chantrele for 4 yeares.
[ ]	Haddam (p^r ditt order [ ] same.
[ ] 97	Paul Leighmans Indnt to Randle Galloway for 9 yea[rs].
	J^{no} Moores Indnt to Randle Gallowa[y] 9 yeares
Jan 3 }	Georg. Worrs of ye County of Lancast App. to Ra[n]dle
[ ]b 7 }	Galloway for Eight Yeares to Virginea or Maryland [ ]now

[1] This list, comprising over 1500 names, is to be found in the back of vols. 5 and 7 of the Records of the Corporation of Liverpool, deposited in the Town Clerk's Office, Leasing Department, Liverpool. The entries were originally arranged chronological-ly, but vol. 5 has been rebound and the pages have been misplaced. The entries are apparently not official, and most of the wri+ing can only be described as scribbling. The writer or writers—the entries seemingly being made by three different scribes—were evidently employed to draw up the indentures. The words "pd." and "deliv-ered" in the margin appear to refer to the indentures, and there is one entry stating that twenty shillings was paid for four indentures.—E. F.

The use of apostrophes at the end of words has been rendered necessary to represent the signs of abbreviation in the original manuscript.

drawn pr. Capt Claytns man.

ditto }
die }
Richd Jones of Carnarvan Apprentice to Randle Galloway for Eight Yeares to Virginia or Maryland this Indent. was drawn p Capt Claytn man.

Janu' : 5 }
97 }
Maudlin Dauis of Ruthin of Wales App' to m^r Wm Webster to Virgin or Maryland for 5 yeares delivered

Katherine Perry of Ruthin to him for ye same time. deliverd.

Joan Rowland of Bangor in Wales to him for ye same time deliv

Richard Jones of Denbyshire for ye same time delid

Edward Jones of Willison in Cheshire for ye same time deli'd

Thomas Cook of Frodsham for ye same time delid

Willm Smith of Dover for 4 yeares delid

Jan' 8. 97. John White of Cicester in Gloucester shire 4 years [delid]

Jno Tonnard of Barbadoes

Not p' 8. 97 Hugh Gryffeth of Denby to Randle Gallowai 4 yeares

Not p' Wm Gryffeth to ye same for ye same time

10 Hugh Partington to Randle Galloway 4 yeares

11 James Walker to ditt 4 yeares

10 J^{no} Thomas of St Asaph to Randl Gall 4 years

20 Hugh Roberts of Anglesay in wales to Jonath Livesey 4 years

20 Jⁿ Gryffin of Carnarv 4 years

Ann Jones of Anglesey to ditt 6 yeares.

To J^{no}. Marshall Mast 'of Y^e Ann And Sarah

Henry Ripley of York	4 years.
Daniel Showland of Cork	4 years
J^{no} Wilson [?] of Nycrofte in Lecestershire	4 years
James Eccles of Loughlavin in Ireland	4 years

J^{no} Steward of London	4 years

April 19–98 Thomas Evans of Denbyshire Carpent. App^r 4 years for Pensylvania to Richd Adams & Wm Lewis

---

For Barbadoes or some of ye Barbba' Islands

May ye 5–1698

Joseph Stile of Talkell Hill[2] Staffordshi' bond' 4 years 6m^o James Gordon

ditto die	Wm English of Fur in Scotland 4 yeares	
ditto die	Samul Wallington of Presbury 4 yeares	
ditto die	Roger Sharples of Lelan' 4 yeares	
ditto die	Richd Hughes of Mould 4 yeares	
May 11–'98	Thom' : Prichard of Beaumaris 7 yeares	
ditto die	Peter Jones of Flintshire 4 yeares	
May 16	J^{no} Prior of Pisor in Flintshire 4 yeares	
June 7–98	Wm Russel of Kinsale 4 yeares	
July 5. 98	Joseph Stile of Staffordshire ap^r m' Gordon	4 4 yeare^s
	Wm English of Scotland	5 4 yeare^s

[2] Talk o' th' Hill.
[3] This entry crossed out.

June 21–98 Jane Horton [or Foster] of Windle Apr. to m' Edw. Tarleton
4 yeares

June 21–98 Rich[d] Cowlund [?] of Thornton Leicastia app[r] to m[r] Gordon
7 yeares—16

William Wilson of Langton in s[d] County to ditto 8 yeares 15

June 27 Jonathan Davis to ditto 4 yeares 4 yeares 19

— 27 Augustine Ca [rr?] 4 yeares 4 yeares 17

— 27 Rich[d] Werton to ditt 4 yeares 4 years 18

July 2[d] 98 J[no] Mason son of J[no] Mason of y[e] Citty of London ⎫
Marrin[r] deceas[d] App[r] to m J[no] Thomas to Vir- ⎬ 7 yeares
ginea or Maryla fr 7 years · Seven Yeares ⎭
W[m] Mason Apr to y[e] same fr. 7 yeares 7 yeares

July 7 '98 William Holt of Preston o[th] Hill in Cheshire Apr' to m ⎫
p' Edward Tarleton to Virgin or Maryland for 4 yeares ⎬ 4
p' Georg Oldham to ditto 4 yeares 4

July 8 to m' James Gordon for Barbadoes Humphry Roberts 7 yeares
11 Carnarvanshire
W[m] Gryffith Cardiganshire 4 yeares 12
Peter Prier Denbyshire 7 yeares 13
J[no] Browne of Lincolnshire Stationer 4 yeares 6
Maurice Roberts of Denbyshire 7 yeares 10
Rich[d] Merton of Denbyshire 7 yeares 9
J[no] Hughes of Merionithshire Sawyer 4 yeares 8
Peter Matthew Denbyshire 4 yeares 7

July 8. 98. Henry Dauis son of Charles Dauis of Denby Apr ⎫
to m[r] Peter Atherton for 4 yeares ⎬ 4 yeares
Jno Roberts Son of Edw[d] Roberts of Queekleys. ⎫
Flintshire ⎬ 4 yeares
J[no] son of J[n] Lloyd of Abergelly Denbyshire 9 yeares

July 19. 98 Laurence Dounes of Maxfield[4] to m[r] Ja : Gordon 4 yeares

July 13. 98 Hugh Powell of Dublin; blacksmith to m[r] Gordon 4 years 14

July 19. 98 Ann Green of Bretherton to m[r] Tarleton for 4 year
Mary Smith of Grosli Parish Flintshire to ditto 4 yea'

July 22 Rich[d] Evans of Carnarvan to m[r] Gordn 4 years 1
Elkana Telson 7 years 2
W[m] Roberts of Denbyshire 4 years 3

July 27. 98 Thomas Lloyd of Cardiganshire to m' Thomas 4 years

27. 98 Watkin Prier of Cardigan to m' Thomas 4 years

July 27. 98 J[no] Harrison of Babington to m' J[no] Thomas to Virginia
8 yeares
W[m] Chanceller of Harbro in Yorkshire to ditto 7 yeares
Rowland Jones of Ruthen to ditto 5 yeares
Elin Cook of London Spinster 5 yeares
Margarett Daughter of J[no] Blake of London to ditt 4 yeares.

[4] Macclesfield.

	J^{no} Bird of Preston in Oxfordshire [*sic*] 4 yeares	
July 29. 98	Gaynold Thomas of Carnarvon to m' Tarletn 4 yeares	
July 29. 98	Thomas Row of Flintshire Taylor apr to m^r Gordon 4 yeares	
Aug 13 1698	Joseph Troughweare of Crosbie in Cumberland Taylor Apr. to m' Henry Brown for Virginia or Maryland for	4 yeares
	Wm Kitchin of Erton in Cumberland Taylor to ditto for 4 yeares	
Augt 17	John Stedman of Padnam^5 Lancaster to m' Edwd Tarlton to Virg for 4 yeares.	
Augt 23	J^{no} Prescott to m^r J^{no} Thomas for	4 yeares
Augt 24	J^{no} Pritchett of Wrexam to m' J^{no} Thomas	7 yeares
	Tho : Powell of Wrexam to ditto	7 yeares
	Hugh Jones of Wrexam to ditto	7 yeares
	Hugh Lealand of Westhoughton to ditto	7 yeares
	Ann Blyth of York Citty Spinst. to ditto	4 yeares
2^d Sept	Thomas Ellis of Dalirauen in Wales to D°	7 yeares

Augst 27	Joseph Reyburne of Waser in Staffordshire shoomaker Appr. to m^r Bryan Blundell for Virginea.	5 yeares
29	Thomas Dunbalin son of Wm Dunbalin to m' Tarleton	6 yeares
29	John Foster of Bethopricke to ditto for	4 yeares
29	John Kirk App to ditto	4 years
29	J^{no} Jones of Wrexham Hannah his Wife and a Child	4 yeares
30 :	Gryffith Thomas Labourer	4 yeares
30 :	Eliz : Markley of Latham	5 years.

Augst 31	Jonas Dauis of Corke to m^r J^{no} Thomas	4 year
31	Richd Owen of Flintshire to ditt	4 year
31	Henry Bond son of James Bond near Garstan to ditt	7 year
Sep^t 2^d	Thomas Ellis of Dalmen in Wales to ditt for	4 year
Sep^t 5	Eliz : King daughter of Abra' King of Dublin to m^r Porter	4 year
	Charity Barlor of Kilkenny to ditto for	5 years
Septr 7th	John Thelfell of Preston Gardiner to m': H: Browne	4 years
7.	J^{no} Dobson of Bolton in Lancashir to ditt	4 year
7 :	Ralph Kettle of Warmingham in Cheshire to ditt	4 year
7.	Henry Bell of Carlisle to ditt	4 years
7.	James Boudler of Ossesstry^6 in Shropshir ditt	4 year
Septr 10	John Owen to John Thomas	4 Years
10	Edwd Jones to D°	4 Years
13	Robert Tongue to m' Henry Browne for	4 Years.
14	Eliz : Wilson of Kirkham in ye fild to m^r Edwd Tarleton	4 yeares
14	Edwd Steele of Westtirlie to m^r Thomas	4 Yeares
14	J^{no} Ducker of Tarvin Taylo. to m' Thomas	4 yeares

^{5} Padiham.
^{6} Oswestry.

| 14 | Richd Darrel of Chester to m' Thomas | 4 years |

14   Richd Darrel of Chester to m' Thomas   4 years
14   Eliz Barlow of Knutsfrd to m' Thomas   4 years
14   Hannah Vaughan of Chester to m' Thomas   4 yeares

---

febru' 17 97   William Ertome of ye Citty of London Apprentice to W^m
            Webster to Virginea or Maryland for 4 year
Jan 28   Jane Evans Denbyshire to m' Webst 5 years deliv^d
Jan 28   Henry Evans Denbyshire 4 yeares deliv^d
Jan 28   Mary Gryffith of Merionthshire 4 years deliv^d
          Ame Watkins Denbyshire 4 year deliv^d
28   Robert Matthew Denby 9 years deliv^d
28   Robert Jones of Denbyshire 4 years delivered

Febr 24th   Elizabeth Jones near Ruthen to m' Webt 5 years deliv^d
          Ann Jones of Rixam 7 delivrd
          Robt Williams near Ruthen 7 delivrd.
          Tho: Davies of Denby 7 delivd
          Mary Tue of Houghtonton [*sic*] in Cheshire 5 deliv^d
          Tho: Babington of Aperton[7] in Cheshire 9
          Joan Williams of Ruthen 5.   deliv^d
          Ellen Hughes of Ruthen 5   deliv^d
          Thomas Owen of Denby 7   deliv^d
          Katherine Hughes of Buthen 5 deliv^d

Feb 28   Richd Edward 4 year of Denby deliverd
deliv^d 2 March 4.97   Wm Bennet of Ashburne Darbyshire deliv^d

---

March 10. 97   Thomas Steward of Widdenbury[8] Chester 7 yeares deliv^d
      10. 97   Thomas Whitaker of Eastquein Cheshire 8 yeares deliv^d
      10. 97   J^{no} Bright Uxbridge Middlesex 4 year deliv^d
      10. 97   J^{no} Dauis of Wopping Middlesex 4 year deliv^d
      10. 97   Georg Baddoe of Clee Shropshire 4 years deliv^d
      10. 97   Edwd Buckley of Bugleton[9] Cheshire 4 year deliv^d
      11. 97   William Dickinson Farn[10] Chesher 4 year deliv^d
      12. 97   Joseph Jinkins of Warton in Chesher 4 year deliv^d

---

March 16. 97   Samuel Low of Nutsford Chesher 4 yeares deliv^d
      16. 97   Thomas Farrel of Dublin 4 yeares deliv^d

March 21.   John Baggeley Apr to Wm Webst^r his selfe 4 year deliv^d
      21.   Joseph Brosier of London [   ] 5 years deliv^d
      21.   John Stol of Sunhen 9 year deliv^d
      21.   Margery Hunt of Knutsford Cheshir 5 year deliv^d
March 23 ⁹⁷/₈
          Henry Prescott of Wigan to m' Wm Webster 4 years delivr^d

[7] Appleton.
[8] Wybunbury.
[9] Buglawton.
[10] Farndon, probably.

delv^d 3^d March 24

        Ann Coulburne of Preston 8 years

delv^d 4.   Peter Fothn' of Tatnal[11] in Cheshir 4 years

March 24 97 fit Hugh Jones of Wrixhan to m' Wm Webster 9 years deliv^d

        fit J^{no} Lloyd of Denbyshire 8 yeares deliv^d

        fit Charles Webster of Denby 8 yeares deliv^d

fit William Hughes of Denbyshire	8	deliv^d
fit Edwd Hughes of Flintshire	9	deliv^d
deliv^d Edwd Howel of St Asaph Flintshire	9	deliv^d
fit J^{no} Morgan of Denbyshire	8	deliv^d
Edwd Roberts of Denbyshire	6	deliv^d
fit Gabriel Roberts of Flintshire	4	deliv^d
fit Thomas Hughes of Ruthen	5	deliv^d
fit Robt Hughes of Denbyshire	4	deliv^d
fit Thomas Roberts of Denbyshire	5	deliv^d
fit Thomas Perrey of Denby	4	deliv^d
Owen Hughes of Ruthen in Wales	8	delivred

April 1 fit 98 Eliz. Roberts of Denbyshire m' Wm Webst^r 7

       fit Margtte W^{ms} of Anglesey 5

       fit Dorathy Edwards Denbyshire 7

       fit James Yates near Blackburn 4

April 13.   Charles Shehy [?] of Dublin 4 yeares deliv^d all

        Thomas Moor of Dublin 4 yeares delid all

        J^{no} Edmunds of Merionthshire 4 yeares del^d all

April 13. 98 Robert Warner of Glocestershire 4 yeares deliv^d

        Thomas Morris of Shropshire 4 years deliv^d

        Richd Worden of Essex 4 yeares deliv^d

Jan 21   Robt Hughes of St Asaph to Mr Webster deliv^d

Jan 21   Wm Ellis of Clantastelh in Wales 7 years deliv^d

Jan 21   John Alvin of Shaftsbery in Dorsetshire deliv^d

Jan 21   John Hughes 7 years deliv^d

Jan 21   William Dauis of Caires in Wales 7 years deliv^d

Feb 18   Thomas Humphrey 9 year Mr Webster deliv^d

Feb 18   Edwd Jones Merionithshire 4 year

Feb 18   Eliz Gryffeth five yeares delivred

Jan 28 97 Richd Jones of Carnarvan to Wm Webster for 4 yeares deliv^d

   28 97 Ann Watkins 4 years

Feb 28   J^{no} Thomas 9 year Denby

Jn 28   Finlh Morris 9 year Denby deliv^d

feb 28   Wm Hughes 9 year Denby deliv^d

Feb 28   Tho Roberts 9 year Denby deliv^d

Feb 28   J^{no} owens Carnarvanshire 6 year deliv^d

Feb 28   Owen Jones of Anglesey 4 year deliv^d

   28   Christian Ireland of Chester 4 years deliv^d

   28   John Jones of Anglesey 4 years deli^d

   28   Henry Perry Montgomerishire 4 year deliv^d

[11] Tattenhall.

Feb 3. 97 Jacob Boulton of Ashton Canes[12] in Wilshire Seu' to m'
Jonatha' Lievsley for three yeares
William Darter Apprentice to ye same for 3 yeares & borne
in ye same Parish
William Prior of Flintshir Apprentice to ye same for 4 year
yeares.

Feb. 16. Henry Brobbin of Warrington 5 yeares to Wm Webster deliv^d
Feb. 16. J^{no} Brobbin ye same tearme deliv^d
Feb 16 Eliz. Brobbin ye same tearme delivrd
Feb 16 Mary Cloud of ye same same tearme deliv^d
Jan. 28 Mary Norman of of Egermun'[13] same tearme deliv^d
Jan. 28 Isabel Troughton of Caton same tearme deliv^d
Feb 16 Mary steel Harperthe in Cheshire same time deliv^d
Jan. 28 Wm Moor of Antrim in Ireland 4 years deliv^d
Feb. 16 Katherine Williams 4 year of Carnarvanshire deliv^d
Jan 28 Mary Williams Flintshire Five yeares delivred

Feb: 18 Robert Clark 4 yeares to m^r Wm Webst^t deliv^d

July 30 98 Mary Jones daughter of J^{no} Jones of Wrixam in Denby-
shire Appr to m' J^{no} Thomas for   4 yeares
August 4. 98 Robt Jones of Denbyshire   4 year
Edwd Jones of Wrixam   7 year
Thomas Duckes of Tarvin in Cheshire   7 year
Mary Cowly hir marke   4 year
9 Robt Faux of Denbyshire   4 year

Augst 10. 98 Henry Jones of Flintshire to m^r J^{no} Thomas for –years
Alice Harlow of Widmore[14] in Herefordshire   4 yeares
Richd Edwards of Cardiganshire   9 years
J^{no} Williams of Cardiganshire   7 years
J^{no} Staton of Congleton Cheshire   9 years
J^{no} Harris of Cardiganshire   7 years.

Augst 16 : 98 Eliz. Jones of Denbyshire to m^r J^{no} Thomas for 5 yeares
17 Rowland Thomas of Anglesey Taylor   5 years
Robt Hughes of Conaway Taylor   4 years
Richd Woods of Adlington Lancashire   7 years
Wm Lawson of Lievsay Lanc.   7 years

Mr. Lewis Jinkin' Servants

Richd Alcock of Bolton Taylor App^r 5 yeares
J^{no} Houseman of Bolton Taylor Apr   5 yeares
Rob : Chalis Castleton in Derbyshire   4 yea
Jo : Bramwale of Preston   4 years
Wm Rycroft of Preston   4 years

[12] Ashton Keynes.
[13] Egremont.
[14] Wigmore.

7br 17	Edward Hardman Apprentice to John Neild of Pen-silvanie to go to Pensilvane for five Yeares	5 Yeares
7b^r 20	Richd Newell to Do for Pensilvane	5 Yeares

7br 19	Tho: Marland to m' Browne	7 Yeares
7b^r 19	John Carneagee of Aberdeene in Scotland to m' Brow^e	4 Yeares
7b^r 20	John Harrison of Ashton under Line to m' Browne	Virginea 7 Yeares
7b 15. 98	Charles Ellis of Macclesfield to m^r Brown	5 Yeares
	Edwd Thorncroft of Sutton in Cheshir to m' Brown	virginea 5 yeares
7b 16	John Davies of Denbygshire Grocer to D^o	4 Yeares
7. 16	Humphrey Howell of Merionethshire to D^o	4 Yeares
7b^r 17	John Wynn of Denbyshire to Henry Browne	5 Yeares
7b^r 20	John Walker of Ashton under Line to m^r Browne	5 Yeares
7b^r 20	John Beecham of Chester to D^o	4 Yeares
7b 20	Thomas Walker of Ashton under Line	7 Yeares
7b 15	Robt Rallestr of Leeds to Richd Bridg for m^r Thomas	4 yeares
7b^r 15	James Jameson of New Castle to m^r Edwd Tarleton	Virginea 4 Yeares
7b^r 17	Robert Pollet son of Robert Pollett late of Bolton to m^r Tarleton	9 Yeares
20	John Nichols to m^r Edward Tarleton	4 Yeares
7b^r 20	Samuell Hemming to DO.	4 Yeares
7b^r 20	John Price of Merionethshire Chirurgeon to m^r Thomas	4 Yeares
7b^r: 22	Thomas Wilding of Litchfield to William Bushell to Virginia	5 Yeares
7b 27	Richd Owen of Carnarvanshire to m^r Thomas	4 Years
7br 27	John Lamb of Levpoole to Ezekiell Parr	4 Yeares
7b' 27	John Ricketts of Lavanshie in Wales to D^o	4 Yeares
d^o die	Jonathan Clarke of Little Mesle in Lan' to m' H. Browne	7 Yeares
27 7b'	Mary Terpin of Lithan in fild to m^r Wm Porter	5 Yeares
28 7b^r	Mary Floyd of Shroesbery in Shropshire to m^r Eze-kiell Parr	5 Yeares
28 7b^r	Jane Hide of Manchest' Spinst' to m' Nicholes Smith	5 Yeares
7b. 30. 98	Matthew Moretown of Presberry in Cheshir to m^r Henry Brown for 4 years	4 years

---

8b. 5.	Robt Voughan son of Thomas Voughan neer Salp. to m^r And. Leed 5 years	

To m^r Nicholas Smith to Virginea Or Maryland
Wm Hudson 5 Yeares October y^e: 13th: 1698
Miles Grimshaw 5 Yeares ditto die.
Mary Boardman 5 Yeares ditto die

8b 17. 98   Tho: Higham of Warrington Toban [?] to m'
        Scarburrough   4 year.

The Names of y^e: Servants that Goes to Virginea in ye Loyalty Capt Henry Browne Commander Octob^r 19th 1698

Ralph Kettle of Warmingham in Cheshire	4 Yeares
Robt: Tongue of Farnoth[15] neare Manchester	4 Yeares
John Threlfell of Preston Gardiner	4 Yeares
Charles Ellis[16] of Macclesfield	5 Yeares
Alexd^r Sinkler of Glascow	4 Yeares
John Wright of Middlesex	4 Yeares
Wm Tayler of Scarbrick	8 Yeares
James Streete	Tenn Yeares
Thomas Walker of Ashton vnder Line	7 Yeares
David Tayler of Mottrom in Cheshir	8 Yeares
John Beecham of Cheshir	4 Yeares
John Walker of Ashton vnder Line	5 Yeares
Georg Low of Gawsworth Cheshir	Tenn Yeares
George Brasfeild	Eleaven Yeares
John Carneagee of Aberdeene in Scotland	4 Yeares
Charles Tayler of Mottrom in Cheshire	7 Yeares
John Harrison of Ashton vnder Line	7 Yeares
Robert Bower[17] of Macclesfeild in Cheshire	7 Yeares
James Bouldler of Augettree[18] in Shropshire	4 Yeares
John Dobson of Bolton Lanc'	4 Yeares
Edwd ThorniCroft of Sutton in Cheshire	5 Yeares
Tho: Marland of Ashton vnder Line	7 Yeares
Humphrey Howell of Merionethshire	4 Yeares
John Davies of Denbigshire Grocer	4 Yeares
Edwd Perry of Denbigshire	4 Yeares
Tho: Vpton of Presberry in Cheshire	Tenn Yeares
John Wynn of Ruthin in Denbigshire	5 Yeares
Jonathan Clark of Little Messin Lanc	7 Yeares
Nathaniel Tayler of Mottrom in Cheshre	9 Yeares
Tho: Tayler of Mottrom in Cheshre	Eleaven Yeares
Mathew Moreton of Presberry Cheshire	4 Yeares
Joseph Troughweare of Crosby in Cumberland Tayler	4 Yeares
Wm Kitchen of Erton[19] in Cumberland Tayler	4 Yeares
Joyce Cooper of Carnarvanshire 4 yeares	4 Yeares
Henry Bell of Carlisle 4	4 Yeares
Tho: Wilding of Litchfield App. (to W^m. Bushell Meate of ye Loyalty) to serve in Virginea for ye Tearme of	5 Yeares
Ja: Barton Apprentice to Janes [sic] Hawkshaw to Monserratt	4 Yeares

---

[15] Farnworth.

[16] A Charles Ellis, son of William Ellis of Macclesfield, was baptized there Aug. 2, 1678.

[17] A Robert Bower, son of Francis Bower of Poynton, was baptized at Prestbury (the mother church of over thirty surrounding townships and chapelries, including Poynton and Macclesfield) 18 Aug. 1678.

[18] Clearly as printed. May stand for Oswestry.

[19] There is a Hutton in Cumberland, for which this may stand.

The Names of all the Servants that Goes to Virginea in the Ship Concord J^{no} Walls Commander October ye 25th 1698 Bound to Ezekiel Parr.

h	Jane Johnson of Wigan Spinster 4 Yeares	
h	Isaac Carpenter 4 Yeares	
h	John Prescot[20] of Wigan Tayler 4 Yeares	
h	Roger Tayler of Abram in ye County of Lanc husband	4 Yeares
h	Oliver Whalley aĩs Wood 7 Yeares	
h	Alice Catterall of Wigan 4 Yeares	
h	Elizabeth Ashton of Wigan Spinster 4 Yeares	
h	Sarah Heyes 4 Yeares	
h	William Scott of Wigan 7 Yeares	
h	Francis Cattarall of Wigan 4 Yeares	
h	John Gasway 4 Yeares	
h	William Fox 4 Yeares	
h	James Exx 4 Yeares	
h	James Butterworth[21] Weaver	4 Yeares
h	John Leyland of Abram Weaver	4 Yeares
h	Mary Moss	4 Yeares
h	Joshua Spencer of vpHolland[22]	7 Yeares
h	Mary Gibbs of Wigan	4 Yeares
h	J^{no} Wood	4 Yeares
h	Alice Heaton	4 Yeares
h	Richd Heaton	4 Yeares
h	Edward Heaton	4 Yeares
h	Margaret Kearfoote of Wigan Spinster	4 Yeares
h	Eliz : Heaton	4 Yeares
	all bound at Wigan ye Countnsts [sic] writt here	
h	Charles Wilkinson of Burnley in Lancashire	7 Yeares
h	Eliz : Rollins of Raiby[23] in Cheshire	4 Yeares
h	Edward Wilson[24] of Tarleton in Lanc	5 Yeares
h	Joseph Stanthrop of Yorkshire Tanner	4 Yeares
h	Ann Eccles of Preston	4 Yeares
h	Charles Coop[25] of Bolton Tayler	4 Yeares
h	James Gambell of Nantwich	4 Yeares
h	Thomas Clayton of Preston	7 Yeares
h	Martha Lloyd of Shroesberry in Shropshire	5 Yeares
h	James Boardman[26] of Bolton Butcher	4 Yeares
h	Thomas Turner of Warrington	4 Yeares
h	Hester Ford of Wigan Spinst^r	4 Yeares
h	Daniel Lyon of Rainford Blacksmith	4 Yeares
h	Thursden Mather of Hinly in Lancashire	4 Yeares
h	James Dangerfeild of Rapahannock River in Virginea	4 Yeares
h	Ellen Peatiason of Fild Lanc'	4 Yeares

[20] John, s. of Thomas Presscot of Daltone, b. 16 Nov., bapt. 22 Nov., 1633 at Upholland, parish of Wigan.

[21] James, s. of Adam Butterworth, bapt. 22 Aug. 1680 at Upholland. Adam Butterworth bur. 25 June 1690 at Upholland.

[22] In the parish of Wigan.

[23] Ribby (?)

[24] Edward, s. of John Wilson of Bretherton, bapt. 10 Apr. 1675 at Croston, of which parish Tarleton was a part.

[25] Charles Coope, s. of Laurence and Elizabeth of Bolton, bapt. 25 Dec. 1674 at Bolton.

[26] James Boardman, s. of Andrew and Deborah of Little Bolton, bapt. 14 May 1676 at Bolton.

h	John Lamb of Leverpoole	4 Yeares
h	John Ricketts Joyner	4 Yeares
h	Eliz: Crompton[27] of Berry in Lanc'	5 Yeares
h	William Thomas of Carnarvanshire	4 Yeares
h	John Johnson of Ipston in Staffordshr Shoomaker	4 Yeares
h	Edward Houghton of Macclesfield	4 Yeares

servants to M' J^n Marsden Merc' who went wth ye Submission

2 9^b 98	Paul Riglie of Hey in Lancashire	7 Yeares
2 9^b	Jeremiah Jones[28] of Berry	7 Years
7	David Bevis of Burstan in Staffordshire	7 Years
7	J^n Newton of Bolton	7 Years
7	Wm Fartley of Orrel near Wigan Husband'	4 Years
7	J^n Winstantly[29] of ye sam husband'	4 Years
7 9^b	Isaac Firth of Bradford in Yorkshire	5 Years
7	Joseph Parr of Little Hilton[30] Lancashire	5 Years

Decem 8 1698 Nath: Fogg bound to Mr Abram Dyson for 4 Years

An Acc^t of ye Servants to Virgin' that went p ye Ann & Sarah m' J^{no} Marshall M^r for Virginea & bound to himself[31]
Novemb. 4. 98 J^{no} Bruin of Chester Shumaker 4 years
Novemb^r 11. 1698.

Tho: Hawkshaw son of George Hawkshaw of Dennam,[32] Cheshire	5 years
Herbert Son of Tho: Patterson late of Chester Chapman	7 yeares
Walter Cramp Son of Wm Cramp of Willington in Shropshire	7 yeares
J^{no} Son of J^n W^{ms} of Widdenbury[33] in Cheshire	5 yeares
Thomas son of Thom^s Jennison late of Lunt in Lancashire	7 yeares
J^{no} son of J^{no} Shaw of Congleton in Cheshire	7 years

An Acc^t of Servants that went to Virginea in ye Ship Lamb of Dublin. m' Wm Burnsides Mast^r

9b. 15. 1698	Judith Butterworth of Middleton in Lancas'	5 yeares
	Sarah Celliam of Manchester	5 yeares
	Ann Sickley of Chadle in Cheshire	5 yeares
	Martha Peak of Broden in Lancash'	7 yeares
	Ann King of Cletherou	5 yeares
	Matthew Newall of Mincheld[34] in Cheshire	7 yeares
	Wm Sheapheard of Manchest	7 yeares

[27] Elizabeth, dau. of William Crompton, b. 15 Apr., bapt. 23 Apr. 1680 at Bury. William, s. of William Crompton, b. 3 Mar., bapt. 12 Mar. 1656-7.
[28] Jeremiah Jones, s. of Richard Jones of the Lees, b. 4 June, bapt. 13 June, 1675 at Bury.
[29] John, s. of Henry Winstanley of Billing, bapt. 11 Apr. 1680 at Upholland, parish of Wigan.
[30] Little Hulton.
[31] This heading and the seven entries under it are crossed out in the original. *Vide infra*, where the list is repeated in somewhat changed form.
[32] Dunham.
[33] Wybunbury.
[34] Minshull.

Jonath' Preestley of Sneland in the County of York 7 yeares
Wm Guy of Duckenfield in Cheshire 5 yeares
Jno Penberry of Manches^r 7 yeares
Rob Leafield of Lancast' 5 yeares
9b ^r 17 Abigail Burnett of Manches^r 5 yeares

An Acc^t of Servants That went to Virginnia in the Shipp Society of Lever-poole Mr Jonath Lievsley Master

Octob^r 23^d. 98 And : Martin of Huttale in Lanc 9 Yeares
John Ramsbotten in County Lanc. 5 Yeares
Novem^r ye 1st John Brown of Cledle[35] Parish Nea Stockport 5 Yeares
2^d Isaac Taylor of Newton in the County of Lanca' 5 Yeares
Eliz^a : Williams of Clutton in ye County of Chester 8 Yeares
Geo : Wisson of Inglewhite in ye County of Lancaster 5 Yeares
4th Mary Clowd of Brewerton[36] in County of Chester 6 Yeares
Jane Banks of Chorley in Lancasher 6 Yeares
11th John Tayler of Coulden in County of Lancashire 5 Yeares
Robt Noblett of Aston Bank in Lancashire 6 Yeares
30th Ayley Blackwell of Brewerton in Cheshire 6 Yeares
Decr 13th Jno Briggs of Waddington in Yorkshire 5 Yeares

Acc^t of Serv^{ts} : y^t Went to Virginnia in ye Globe Mr Simpson Master

Decr ye 2^d John Strachine of Scotland 4 Years
3 Alexander Marsh of Aughton Lancashire 8 Yeares
Homer Rodan of Scotland to Mr Neilson 4 Yeares
Pd for James Douglass of Scotland D^o 4 Yeares
5 Peter Holland of Middle Witch 6 Yeares
15 James Corry of Scotland 4 Years

1698 An Acc^t of Servants Thatt went to Virginnia in the good Shipp Called the St John Baptest : Mr Nicholas Franch.

October 24th John Thompson of Cumberland 7 Yeares
John Rudd of Liverpoole Webster 4 Yeares
Peter Winstanley[37] of Oriell 4 Yeares
Abram Rudd of Rachdale Clothier 4 Yeares
John Gilburt of Holtbridge in Essex 4 Yeares
John Morgan of Apsom[38] 4 Yeares
John Fisher of Holmes Chappell 4 Yeares
Samuell Williams of Wrixham 10 Yeares
William Collins of Bristoll 4 Yeares
Thomas Williams of Wrixham 10 Yeares
Robert Lewis of Denbyshire 4 Yeares
John Redding of Canterbury 4 Yeares
Daniell Child of Whitechappele 4 Yeares
Richard Lewis of Branford 4 Yeares
Robert Finch of Wrixham 10 Yeares

---

[35] Cheadle(?)
[36] Brereton(?)
[37] Peter Winstonle, s. of John of Orrel, bapt. 26 Dec. 1669 at Upholland. John, s. of Thomas Winstanley of Billing, bapt. 13 Sept. 1646 at Upholland.
[38] Epsom, Surrey(?)

	Elizabeth Holding of Lanc Spinster	4 Yeares
26th	Caelia Woods of Berry in Lanc	6 Yeares
	Elizabeth Hunt of Wrixham	4 Yeares
	Ruth Davies of Wrixham Spinster	4 Yeares
	Henry Woods of Derry	4 Yeares
28	Alexander Challinor of Macclesfield	4 Yeares
	Ann Evans of Wrixham	4 Yeares
Novem ye 18	Edward Clark of Uttertter[39] in Stafford	4 Yeares
	Edward Williams of Rixam	4 Yeares
	John Taylor of Wellington in Shropshire	4 Yeares
28	John Cheetum of Oldham in the County of Lancaster	4 Yeares
	Jam Pye of Lyddgate in the County of Lancaster	4 Yeares
29th	Margt Renndle of Pilling, Indentd to John Fox, Mate of the sd shipp,	7 Yeares
Decr 5	Newman Steward of the County of Norfolk	4 Yeares
31	William Hodgkins to m' Conly of Blackly in Worcetsh'	4 Yeares

An Acct of Servts That Went to Virginnia in the Ann and Sarah Mr John Marshall Master
Novem: 4th: 98

	John Bruin of Chester	4 Yeares
7	Michl Godwin of Winchester	4 Yeares
11	Jno Shaw of Congleton in Chesshire	7 Yeares
	Tho: Jennyon of Lunt in Lancashire	7 Yeares
	Jno Williams of Chesshire	5 Yeares
	Walter Crampton [40] of Willington in Shropshire	7 Yeares
	Herbert Patterson of Chester Chapman	7 Yeares
	Thos: Hawkshaw of Dannam [41] in Cheshire	5 Yeares
16th	Jno Hoague of Cload in Cheshire	9 Years
19th	Wharton Fallowfield of Pennyroth[42] in Cumberland	4 Years
24	William Wood of Tarvin in Cheshire	5 Yeares
26	Jno Lloyd of Weppen in Flintshire	8 Years
Decr 2	Jno Lyon of Huntspear in Somersetshire	4 Yeares
5	Jno Baker of Astberry in Cheshire	5 Yeares
7	Jno Shaw of Millhouse in Lancashire	4 Yeares
9	Wm Heaton of Heaton in Lancashire	4 Yeares
10	Job: Howard of Sawford by Manchester	5 Yeares
	Ann Dumbile of Middle Witch in Cheshire	4 Yeares
	Sarah Pinkston of Do	4 Yeares
16	Jno Rothell of Toddington[43] in Lancas':	5 Yeares
16th	Samll Mccreky of Carlisle in Cumberland	5 Yeares
	Elisa: Valentine of Leverpoole	6 Yeares
20th	Dan: ll Walker of Stand of Polkington in Lancashire	4 Yeares
22d	Joseph: Brosents of Burnby in Lancashire	4 Yeares

[39] Uttoxeter(?)
[40] The ton of Crampton has been added and crowded in. *Vide ante* for the original form of the list.
[41] Dunham.
[42] Penrith.
[43] Tottington.

| | Adam Mottershed[44] of Macclesfield in Cheshire | 4 Yeares |
| 23 | John Milener of Holebrook in Yorkshire | 5 Yeares |

An Acc[t]: of Servants That went to Virginnia in the Ship Called the Eleanor of Liverpoole Nicholas Reynolds Master Septem[r]: 5 : 1698

	Charles Barber of Kilkenny	5 Yeares
	Elizabeth King of Dublin	4 Yeares
	Martha Jackson bound but remaned	4 Yeares
24th	John Pennant of flintshire	7 Yeares
27	Mary Terpin of Lathom in field	5 Yeares
October 18	John Posthous of Harding in Wales	5 Yeares
19	Ralph Haliwale of Bolton falsified his name it was Thoms	4 Yeares
22	Diana Johnson[45] of Presberry in Chesshire	4 Yeares
	Marg[t] Bantum of Coppl in Lancashire	4 Yeares
	Mary Smallwood of Bartumlee in Cheshire	4 Yeares
Novem[r] 2[d]	Peter Shellom of Presberry in Cheshire	7 Yeares
	Thomas Upton of Presberry d[o]	4 Yeares
Gone [crossed out]		
	Martha Jackson[46] of Presberry d[o]	5 Yeares
	John Upton[47] of D[o]	5 Yeares
	Elizabeth Upton of D[o]	4 Yeares
4th	Susanna Pound of Devon Widdowe	4 Yeares
7th	John Haggarty Ireland	4 Yeares
19th	William Beck of Underbarraugh in Westmoreland	4 Yeares
	Rob[t] Lawson of Burnick in Lanccshire	4 Yeares
	Rich[d] Holmes of Preston in Lanca :	4 Yeares
	Peter Jones of Anglesey	4 Yeares
	Hugh Owen of Anglesay	4 Yeares
	William Owen of Anglesay	4 Yeares
22[d]	James Morden of Bristoll	7 Yeares
28	Elizabeth Wilson of Carleton in County of Lancas :	4 Yeares
29	John Hartopp of Coventry	4 Yeares
30	John Porter of Wimsley[48] Parish in Chesshire	4 Yeares
Novem[r]: 17th :	James Barbur bound to John Tyrer	7 Yeares
Dec[r] 2[d]	Katherine Ritchley of Ayre in Scotland	
3 :	W[m] Blundell of Cheedley Holme[49] in Cheshire	5 Yeares
9th	Rp[h]. Relshaw of Lendy in Yorkshire	7 Yeares

An Acc[t] of Servants that went to Virginea in the Ship Barbadoes Merc[t] and were bound to m' Cuthbert Sharples

23–9b 98	Josiah Mayeres of Macklesfield in Cheshire	4 Yeares
23	Jane Swindle of Maxfield Mem[d] She was bound to Aldem[n] Houghton	5 Yeares
25	Thomas Yates of Whiston	5 yeares

[44] Adam, s. of Roger Mottersheade of Mottram, bapt. 7 Aug. 1677 at Prestbury, of which parish Macclesfield was also a part.
[45] Dyana, dau. of John Johnson of Falibroome, bapt. 4 Feb. 1678-9 at Prestbury.
[46] Martha, dau. of Peter Jackson, bapt. 1 Feb. 1681 at Prestbury.
[47] John, s. of James Upton of Newton, bapt. 28 Jan. 1679-80 at Prestbury.
[48] Wimbersley.
[49] Cheadle Hulme.

25	Aaron Summers of Kellen in Lancash[r]	5 yeares
25	W[m] Davies of Mosteyn in Flintshire	5 yeares
1 xb	J[no] France of Huddorsfield in Yorkshire	4 yeares
1 :	Elizabeth Dickin of Denby in Wales	4 yeares
1 :	Mary Holme[50] of Bolton	4 yeares
2. 9b.	Joyce Cooper of Carnarvanshire	4 yeares
1. xb	Mary Case[51] of Bolton	4 yeares
1	Sarah Gibbons of Maclesfield	4 yeares
2	Benjamin Roy[l] [52] of Macklesfield	7 yeares
28.8b	Samuel Dagnell of S[t] Hellen in Lancash[r]	5 yeares
xb. 5	W[m] Cragge of Dent in Yorkshire	5 yeares
12	Rob[t] Ward of Bolton in Lancashire	6 Yeares

An Acc[t] of Serv: [ts] That Went to Virginnia in the Shipp Called the Submission of Leverpoole Thomas Seacome Master Octob[r] : 7 : 1698

William Relict of Gatle-mellit in Flintshire	Bound	4 Yeares
John Young of Wandsor in Surrey	To M[r] John	4 Yeares
William Bradshaw of Long Green in Chesshire	Hughes	4 Yeares
12th John Adams of Shotten in Flintshire		4 Yeares
14th John Thompson of Coalrain in Ireland	Bound to	4 Yeares
Henry Woods of Chester	M[r] Jn[o] Hughes	4 Yeares
24th Mary Standish of Stafford, Spinster		4 Yeares
Mary Faulkner of Manchester, Spinster		4 Yeares
Martha Newton of Macclesfield		4 Yeares
25th Joan Witter of Tapperly in Chesshire		4 Yeares
28th Philip Finn of Harding Parish in Wales		4 Yeares
John Finn of D[o]		6 Yeares
Novem[r] : 2[d] Robert Middleton of Oacks Parish in Derby Shire		4 Yeares
Ellin Barlow of Macclesfeild in Cheshire		4 Yeares
Tho : Williams of Carnarvan in Wales		5 Yeares
Fran : Glanford of Buckinhamshire		4 Yeares
And : Hamilton of Edenborough		4 Yeares
16th Rich[d] Fin near harding in Flintshire		4 Yeares
23 William Pelkington[53] of Brindle		5 Yeares

Acc[t] of Servants that Went to the West Indies in the Ann and Mary, John Dann Master, and bound to him, 169⁸/₉

March the
28: 169⁸/₉   Thomas Roper of Wrightingham in Lancashire
Aged (19) Yeares bound for   4 Yeares

[50] Mary Holme, dau. of Timothy of Little Bolton, bapt. 25 Apr. 1680, Marah Holme, dau. of Jas. and Margaret of Bolton, b. 29 Nov., bapt. 2 Dec., 1677 at Bolton.
[51] Mary Care, dau. of Samuel and Martha of Bolton, b. 29 Nov., bapt. 2 Dec., 1677 at Bolton.
[52] Benjamin Royle, s. of Henry Royle, bapt. 30 Sept. 1673 at Macclesfield.
[53] William Pilkington, s. of John, bapt. 17 Feb. 1680-1 at Brindle. John Pilkington and Agnes Waring m. 24 July 1676 at Brindle. John Pilkington churchwarden of Brindle in 1679.

Aprill the 4th:Henry Halewood of Ormskirk in Lancashire
Aged (25) Yeares bound for   4 Yeares

Mem^d if Peter Atherton of Cuerdly aged about Ten Yeares Comes to Offer himself he is apprentice to Tho: Richardson of the same place. A Gray Wastecoat, & Gray Stockings a Jockey Capp: Flaxen hair'd

---

Acc^t of Servants bound to Mr Wm Middleton Master of the Irish Lawrell of Leverpoole bound for Newfoundland as Viz^t:

Feb: 21 1$\frac{699}{700}$ [Age] [Term]

		Age	Term
	Henry Powell of Wells in Sommersetshire	21	– 4
	James Tucker of Wells	20	– 4
	Thomas Jones of Carnervan	20	– 4
Runn	Thomas Jackson of Blakeley in Lanc'	19	– 4
Feb: 27	Wm Williams of Narbot in Pembrookshire	21	– 4

Acc^t of Servants bound to Capt Edwd Tarleton and Went to Newfoundland in the (Yorkshire) Lawrell of Leverpoole as Viz^t:

Feb^{ry}: 27 : 1$\frac{699}{700}$

	Evan Owen of Ossesstry[54] in Shropshire	20	– 4
	Thomas Williams of Carnarvan in Wales	12	– 9
28th	Hugh Reddish of Kearsly Near Bolton in Lanc'	19	– 4
	John Stock of Rachdale in Lanc'	23	– 4
	John Barnes of Hazledine[55] in Lanc'	15	– 7
	John Wood of D^o	13	– 8

John Bretherton of Nantwich in Cheshire   20 – 4

Acc^t of Serv^{ts} that Went to New England in the Virginnia Merch^t Edmund Ball Master 1699

Imp^{rs}: Mar: 3^d 99

	years of Age	Yeares to serve
Jane Radcliff of Rachdale in Lancashire Spinster	20	7
Mary Gleddale of Hepworth in Yorkshire	20	7
Danill Clows of Osterfield in Staffordshire	23	6
John Holgrave of Hazledine[56] in Lancashire	28	7
James Nuttes of Blakebourne d^o	18	7
Paul Widdop of Hallifax in Yorkshire	26	7
John Walker of Tithrton[57] in Cheshire	19	7
Christophr Patrick of Great Musgrove in Westmoreland	20	7
Mathew Mooreton[58] of Presbury in Cheshire	20	7
John Jones of Clanderry Denbyshire Wales	17	7
James Thompson of the Kingdom of Scotland	19	7
Josiah Maires of Macclesfield in Cheshire	19	7

---

[54] Oswestry.
[55] Haslingden.
[56] Haslingden.
[57] Titherington.
[58] Matthew, s. of Matthew Moreton, bapt. 22 Nov. 1676 at Prestbury.

	Mary Dawson of Leades in Yorkshire	22	7
	Margaret Jones of Ritchin in Denbyshire	32	7
	James Chaddock of Rotchdale in Lancashire	22	7
	Jane Swindle of Macclesfield in Cheshire	23	7
	Edward Cook of Hope Parish in Derbyshire	19	7
	Richard Thomas of Dublin in Ireland	18	7
	Nicholas Hurd of Possenby[59] in Cumberland	19	7
	Thomas Stringer of Buckton in Yorkshire	22	7
	John Beaver of Hepworthe in Yorkshire	22	7
	Jonath: Hartly of Martown in Yorkshire	18	7
	Edward Glover of Manchester in Lancashire	20	7
	Hugh Hughles [sic] of Anglesey in Wales	19	7
	Peter Bole of Paynton in Cheshire	20	7
	Margarett Todd of Ingleton in Yorkshire	19	7
	Mary Tayler of Ratchdale in Lancashire	22	7
	James Clarke of Newtown heath in Cheshire	17	7
	Edward Faux of Flint in Wales	19	7
	Math: Williams of Blew Morrice in Wales	26	7
	Humph Salsbury[59a] of Glandiray in Denbyshire	19	7
	Marg^t Bishop of Loughbourough in Lecestershire	25	7
	Peirce Tickle[60a] of Limb in Cheshire	17	10
	John Smith of Craven in Yorkshire	17	7
Turnd off	John Williams of Woolwich in Kent	29	7
4th	John Roadly of the City of Norwich	17	7
6	Dan^ll Clew of Manchester in Lancashire	21	7
	John Rothett of Blackbourn in Lancashire	19	7
	Maudlin Lewis of Carmarthen Town in Wales	15	7
Turnd off	John Mills of Oldham in Lancashire	12	10
Run	{ Joseph Bell of New Castle upon Tine	23	7
	{ Lawrence Scotland of Scotland	21	7
	Ann Singleton of Firwood[60] in Lancashire bound to Mr John Moody	23	7

An Acc^t: of Servants that went to Pensilvania, Virginnea or Marly in the good Ship the Experiment of Leverpoole Cavaleiro Christian Master; all bound to Mr John Hughes of the s^d Ship Aug^s: 16. 1699

		Yeares of Age	Yeares to serve
June 20th : 1699	Mary Lee of Peake in Derbyshire Spinster	19	6
	Richard Worrall of Bridget Parish in the City of Chester Tayler	21	5
July 4th	Stephen Fletcher of the City of London Taylor	21	6
	William Windsor of Potters Marson in Leicestershire Blacksmith	18	6
July 11	James Johnson of Sawford in Lancashire Weaver	23	5
	Ellin Acres of Sephton in Lancashire		

59 Ponsonby.
59a Humphry Salsbury and Mary Milborn m. at Boston, Mass., 11 July 1707.
60a Peirce Tickle and Jane Ratleife m. at Boston, Mass., 26 May 1707.
60 Firgrove (?)

	Spinster	22	6
	Ellin Rushton of Whaley Parish in Lancashire	18	6
July 20th	George Griffith of Colin[61] in Flintshire	23	6
22^d	Marg^t Plaise of Stairbourne in Yorkshire	20	6
	John Rhodes of Hallifax Parish in Yorkshire Weaver	21	5
Aug^s: 4th	Marg^t Ellis of Merryonithshire in Wales	28	5
	Wm Ellis of the same	26	5
	Elizabeth Wharton of Frodsham Parish in Cheshire	22	6
	Jane Lackey of Carrickfargus in Ireland	18	5
Aug^s: 9th	John Jones of Northey in Flintshire	28	5
15th	John Richard of Clanarman Parish in Denbyshire	16	7

M^{dm} Richard Berlow Apprentice to Wm Hoome of Manchester Dyer Ou [*sic*] Runn his Master Aug 22 : 1699. to Send a note to his s^d Master to Enquire whether he is Consenting to his Goeing to Sea or not.

Servants Bound to Mr Richard Murfey Master of the Lamb of Doblin Bound to Verginnia

Septemb^r 4° 1699 :

		Age
	Phebe Leed of Oldham in Lancashire	19–05
do	Robert Owen of Seale in Cheshire Taylor	18–05
do	Mary Speakman of Clifton in Lancashire	20–05
do	Thomas Lindsay of Pendleton in Lancashire	16–09
do	Ellen Holt of Rachdale in Lancashire	27–05
6°	John Andrew of Oldham in Lancashire	22–04

Septr 19° }	Mary Atkinson of Nottingley in Yorkshire	21–5
1699 }	Bound to M^l Henry Smith of Liverpoole Merch^t	
9 br 20°: 99	Joseph Elwood of Garston Taylor To Henry Smith	19–4

October	John Nuttong of Burnley in Lancashire to Mr Robert	
7°: 1699	Fleetwood	12–10

To Mr Lewis Jenkins

	Richard Edwards of Denbyshire	14–7
9 ber 9°	John Edward d°	18–5
1699	Robt Powell d°	20–6
	Robt Davies	21–6

		Age	Yeares
Septr 12th	John Nicholson of Lancaster bound to Mr Thomas Tyler to go to new England for Seaven Yeares	20	– 7
14°	John Thomas of Clandethlow in Carmarthenshire bound to Capt Clayton for ye West Indies	18	– 7

[61] Colwyn (?)

Servants bound to Thomas Bowling of Exton in Lancashire husbandm':
Octobe 14°: And Went in the Elizabeth for Viginniae or Maryland: Gilbert Leivsay Master

		age	
Octob^r: 14°	James Hall of Exton in Lancashire	11	12
1699	Joshua Holden of Heath Charnock in Lancashire	16	08
P^d	Thomas Colson of Chorley	18	08
	William Dickinson of Flucton in Yorkshire	14	08
	William Conly of Ouse Walton in Lancashire	09	13

Serv^{ts}: Bound to Mr Bryan Blundele Mast^r of the Mulberry October the 24°: 1699

8ber 24°: 99 {	Isaac Scofield of Chatherton[62] near Manchester	13:11
	James Scofield his brother	11:11
	Edward Lunt of Maile[63] in Lanc'	13:11

8ber 26:99   William Scott of Portsm° to Mr John Parker   14:07

9ber. 10   Jacob Rylance of Morley in Cheshire to Richard Singleton   24:5

Servants Bound to Mr Henry Brown Master of the Loyalty bound for Virginnia or Maryland

		Age
8ber 24°: 99	Francis Boardman of Gorton near Manchester	21–4
	Ann Williams of Denbyshire	22–7
	Jam: Kershaw of Blakely in Lanc'	18–7
	Wm Kinder of disley in Cheshire	16–7
	Math Stabbs Sen of Rushton in Staffordshire	44–6
	Math Stabbs jun' of Ditto	15–9
	Edward Stabbs of Ditto	16–8
	Ewen Lommas[64] of Bury in Lanc^r	21–5

An Acc^t of Servants bound to Mr Wm Porter of Leverpoole Merchant and went in the Shipp Eleanor for Virginnia or Maryland Mr Nicholas Reynolds Master 1699

Jan^{ry} 2th 1699	Constant Jeoffrys of St Asaphs in Wales	16–5
3^d	Elizabeth Edwards of Yarmouth	18–5
10	Charles Quarryer of Sandbich in Cheshire	25:4

---

[62] Chadderton (?)
[63] Mill or Meols (?)
[64] The following items refer to Bury: Owen, s. of John Lommas, b. 19 Apr., bapt. 27 Apr., 1679. John, s. of Richard Lomax, Taylor, b. 24 Mar., bapt. 28 Mar., 1650. John, s. of Richard Lomax, Elton, b. 28 July, bapt. 6 Aug. 1648. John, s. of Richard Lomax, Goosford, b. 4 Sept., bapt. 12 Sept., 1647. Wife of Richard Lomax, Taylor, d. 2 Oct., bur. 3 Oct., 1652. Richard Lomax, Taylor, d. 12 May, bur. 13 May, 1651. Anne, w. of Richard Lomax, Cooper, d. 28 June, bur. 30 June, 1651-2. Wife of Richard Lomax, Carpenter, bur. 27 Apr. 1661. Richard Lomax, Shipobotham, d. 15 Mar., bur. 18 Mar., 1671-2. Izabell, wife of Richard Lomax, d. 5 July, bur. 7 July, 1673. John Lomax and Esther Howorth, both of Bury, m. 13 Feb. 1671-2. John Lomax and Elizabeth Greenhalgh, m. 12 Aug. 1672. John Lomax and An Low of Bury m. 7 Jan. 1672-3. Jo^n Lomax Curate of Bury in 1694. John Lomax Churchwarden in 1685. Richard Lomax of Redwells Churchwarden in 1651. Esther, dau. of James Howorth of Elton, b. 7 Mar., bapt. 13 Mar. 1650. Elizabeth, dau. of John Greenhalgh, Catholic, b. 19 Nov., bapt. 24 Nov., 1653.

	Mary Steele of Beeston Castle in Cheshire	25 : 4
	Jane Wright of Skipton in Yorkshire	15 : 7
	Mary Anderton of Leverpoole in Lancashire	20 : 4
19th	John Travers of Denbyshire	14 : 7
	Mary Jones of Carnarvan in Wales	18 : 5
20th	Samwell Smallwood of London & his Wife Martha	35 : 27 : Each 4
	Wm Huntington of Middlewich in Cheshire	28 : 4
	Ellen Masterman of Ornskirk	20 : 5
	Eliz^{a.} Galliburn of Blackbourn	18 : 5
	Tho : Hodgkinson of Preston	19 : 4
	Math. Thorp of the City of York	24 : 4
	John Thorp of Mossen near Manchester	13 : 8
	Steph Thomas of Twissock in Denbyshire	15 : 7
	Edward Jones near Wrexham in Wales	20 : 7
Feb : 9 :	Richard Dalton of Carlisle in the County of Cumberland	26 : 4
19	David Curran of the City of Dublin	30 : 4

---

¹⁶⁹⁹/₁₇₀₀

Serv^{ts} : bound to Mr John Rimmer Master of the Good Ship Planter bound for Newfoundland Mar : 18° : 1699.

| March ye 18th | James Day of Doublin in Ireland | 22–5 |
| | James Garnette of Rainhill in Lanc' | 22–5 |

Serv^{ts} : Bound to Wm Benn Master of the Elizabeth and Ann bound for Montserratte in the West Indies

March ye 19° ⁹⁹/₇₀₀	Lawrence French of Galloway in the Kingdome of Ireland	26 : 4
	William Spence of Cambridg	20 : 5
	John Lindsey of Ballenmenough in the County of Antram Ireland	18 : 9
	Robert Joyce of Tane in the County of Galloway in the Kingdom of Ireland	25 : 4
March 26. 1700		
	Wm Thompson of London Marr'	31 : 4
	Thom^t : Pickering of Great Budworth in Cheshire	29 : 4
	William Davies of Belfast	24 : 4
	Richard Messenger of Creeklard[65] in Wiltshire	31 : 4

To Mr Gravill Parifie

| Apr^{le} : 20° : 1700 | Richard Jones[66] Bury in Lanc' | 15 : 9 |

An Acc^t of Servants Bound to Mr Peter Atherton and Mr Richard Bridg for Acc' of s^d Mr Peter Atherton to go in ye good Ship Lamb to Vir ginea or Maryland : and Shipt on board hir this the 8th day Septem^r 1699.

July 14. 99	Wm Evans of Denbyshire aged 23 yeares	23– 5 yeares
	Andrew Pritchett of Carnarvanshire aged	23– 5 yeares
	Thomas Berkett of Kendall	17– 7

[65] Cricklade.
[66] Richard, s. of Richard Jones de Leeys, b. 25 Mar., bapt. 1 Apr., 1687 at Bury.

Wm Hubbart of Hilmartin Parish, Wiltshire   21– 4
Thomas Barlow of Manchester   19– 5
J^no Jones of Northrop Flintshire   19– 5
Tho: Hughes of Denbyshire   14– 9
Hugh Robert of Denby Town   13–10
Wm Gryffith of Rathbone near Wrexham   13–10
Peter Évans neer Denby   14–10
Hugh Morris of Little Church in Denby   14–10
Robert Price of Denby Town   13–11
Peter Dauis of Denby   13–11
Henry Parrey of Olky in Flintshire   20– 1
J^no Dauis of Denby Town   13–11
Wm Roberts of Grandyel in Denbyshire   14– 9
Wm Williams of Denby Green in Wales   14–10
Tho: Owen of Abergelly[67] in Denby-
shire   25– 5
J^no Dauis of Denby Town aged   28– 5
Lewis Jones of Beaumauris   30– 5
Jane French of Holme near Lancas'   21– 4
Edwd Guy of Aughton in Lancashire   34– 5
Margarette Lloyd of Denby Town   20– 4
Evans Hughes of Anglesey   13– 8
Edwd Bumber of Denbyshire   14–10
J^no Williams of Denbyshire   12–10
Robert Edwards of Merionithshire   22– 5
J^no Morrice of Denbyshire   16– 9
Richd Williams of Denbyshire   12–11
Hugh Pierce of Denbyshire   35– 6
Martha Hughes of Denbyshire   17– 5
Ann Sammell of Meryonithshire   15– 7
Richd Jones of Denbyshire Taylor   19– 7
David William of Denbyshire   21– 5
Joseph Hart of Warwychshire   16–10
Benjamin Bagshaw   12– 9
Maurice Jones of Denbyshire   17– 7
Richard Edwards of Denbyshire   19– 6
J^no Gryffith of Denbyshire   17– 7
Aug' 5   Richd Stannor of Northwich Cheshire   17– 8
11   Peirce Hughes of Molleyn   15– 9
Margarette Jones of Carnarvanshire   17– 5
Aug^st 19   Richd Tomlinson of Waddington in Yorkshire   31– 5
Mary Taylor of Brurton[68] wood   34– 4
Thomas Howarth of Limb in Suffolk Taylor   21– 4
21   J^no Dene of ye Citty of London   14– 7
Richd Faulkner of Ludlow in Shropshire   15– 7
Mary Whitaker of Manchester   21– 4
Alice Diggles of Eccles Parish   27– 4
Joseph Crosbie of Nassburrough in Yorkshire   24– 5
24   Wm Barton of Scazebrick   28– 5
Richd Hughes of Denbyshire   14– 8

[67] Abergele.
[68] Brereton (?)

	J^{no} Thomas of Merionithshire	10–12
	Gryffith Arthur of Denbyshire	21– 5
	Wm Edmunds of Denbyshire	12–12
	Tho: Francis of Carnarvanshire	24– 5
	J^{no} Morris of Carnarvanshire	20– 6
	Thomas Lloyd of Flintshire	13– 8
	Margarette Evans of Carnarvanshire	18– 5
	Nathaniel Waring of Floor in Northamptonsh	37– 5
7b. 4	Evan Roberts of Denbyshire	15–10
	Henry Owen of Abergelley parish in Denby	38– 5
	Elizabeth Thomas of Anglesey	26– 4
	Ann Owen of Abergelly	38– 5
	Rowland Thomas of Anglesey	34– 4
	William Dauis of Cothelwell in Meryonthshire	19– 5
	Edwd Farrington of Chester Watchmaker	20– 5
	J^{no} Fuller of Market Drayton in Shropshire blacksmith and Mary his Wife	26– 4
	Jacob Sherwood of Okingham in Cheshire	13– 8
	Henry Proctor of Walton	16– 7
	Richard Barlow of Manchester ran away	20– 6
	J^{no} Cartwright of Manchester ran away	19– 6

Acc^t of Serv^{ts}: bound to Mr John Walls Mast^r: of the Concord bound for Virginnia or Maryland December the 7°: 1699.

8ber: 25°: 99	Joseph Monk of Clayton i'th Moores in Lanc: Carpent'	22 : 4
	Jennet Monk his Wife	26 : 4
	Eleazer Fletcher of Leades in Yorkshire	25 : 4
	Robert Twiddale of Fixby in d^o	23 : 4
	Ann Harrison of Scazbrick	19 : 5
	Marg^t Corrwinn of London	20 : 4
	Ann Richardson of Wallesley	20 : 4
	Elizabeth Cave of Warten Moore near Manchester	27 : 4
	Eliza Hunter of St. Albans Denbyshire	12 : 9
	Wm Hall of Burnley in Lanc'	21 : 4
	J^{no} Walker of Henley	19 : 4
	Wm Preston of Wittenborow[69] in Chester	22 : 4
	Eleanor Drury of Shrewsberry	23 : 4
	Richard Shaw of Ratchdale	21 : 4
	Thom' Connily of London	26 : 4
	Jane Bennet of Sutton in Cheshire	23 : 6
	John Jones of Llandurneugh in Denbyshire	13 : 9
Runn	Patk Dunkin of Sneeton in Yorkshire husbandm'	35 : 4
	Marg^t Lamb of Dalton in Lancashire	21 : 6
	John Leasiter of Hotsfield[70] in Cheshire	22 : 4
	Wm Snalshaw [sic][71] of upholland in the County of Lanc'	22 : 4
16 : xb. 99	Richd Haddock of Lealand aged 14 yeares	14 : 11
xber 28	Edwd Warrington of Macclesfeild	27 : 5

[69] Wybunbury (?)
[70] Hoofield (?)
[71] Probably Smalshaw, a name frequently found in the Registers of Upholland.

	Wm Thomas of Carnarvanshire	35 : 5
	John Harrisson of Denbyshire in Wales	21 : 5
Jan. 3	Tho Hughes of Holliwell	25 : 5

December the first James Ridgway of Prestbury in Cheshire to Capt
Wm Clayton for the Island of St Kitts Aged 22 :   3 bound

Dec^r : 16th : 99 { John Woods (a Poor Child) of Aughton in Lancashire by Consent of the Overseers of Aughton afores^d. To Capt Clayton for Seaven Yeares at St Kitts in the West Indies Joshua Taylor d^o of D^o by D^o to D^o for Tenn Years at St Kitts   Richard Latham and Thomas Harker Overseers

Maurice Griffith enquired for ye 26 2b 99
James Holme of Ormeskirke Taylor

Bound to Mr Jonath Leivsay

		Age	Yeares
Septemb^r : 25° 1699 }	Charles Mills[72] of Bury in Lancashire	16	8
October 11	Margarett Hughes of Anglesay in Wales	22	5
d^o	Katherine Maddock of the City of Chester	16	8
Novem^r 25°	George Holt of Hallifax in Yorkshire	17	7
d^o	Robert Reynolds of Clanledon in Denbyshire	19	6
d^o	George Reynolds of d^o	17	6
d^o	Evan Edwards of Ebellah in Merryonithshire	26	5
d^o	Wm Humphrey of Beltworth in d^o	16	8

Bound to Mr William Fletcher

1699			
xber 20	James Seacome of Preston Patrick in Westmoreland	20 : 8	
Jan^{ry} : 27	Peter Holland of Conway in Denbyshire	26 : 4	
Feb : 2	Thomas Phithian of Mossen in Cheshire	28 : 4	
Feb : 6	J^{no} Lethberrie of Hilton in Darbyshire Carpenter	22 : 4	
ead die	Tho : Lethberrie of y^e same husbandm'	25 : 4	

Bound to Mr Lawrence Thompson p Acc^t of Mr Houghton
April 10th 1700

	Anth^o Stuart of Scotland	34 : 5
	Jonath Crimes of Sandyway in Cheshire	21 : 5

Bound to M' Samuel Waring

	Nicholas Brooke of Stradford in Lanc	12 : 9
	Joseph Munck of Hazleinden[73] Husb$\overline{m}$	22 : 4

Acc^t. of Servants That went to Virginia With Mr Gilbert Leivsay [   ]
the [   ] 1699 in the Elizabeth of Leverpoole

72 The following items refer to Bury : Charles, s. of John Mills, b. 12 May, bapt. 21 May, 1682. John, s. of John Mills, b. 19 Jan., bapt. 4 Feb., 1657–8. John Mills of Walmersley in the parish of Bury and Sarah Greggory in the parish of Ratlife m. at Newhall 19 May, 1656.
73 Haslingden.

	Age	Servd years
Elizabeth Addison of Kirby Staven[74] in Westmoreland	24	05
Mary King of Leverpoole	24	05
James Syddale of Ellingborough in Lancashire	18	06
Sarah Allison of Cuerdly dᵒ	24	04
Adam Simner[75] of Lealand	19	04
William Water of Walton le dale in dᵒ	17	05
Margᵗ Lavinsley of Wrighton	19	07
John Brascoup of Burnley	18	05
Abram Scowfield of Manchester	23	05
Ann Kirkome of Gorome Hills	23	04
Jane Willington of Barton	21	04
Adam Leasiter of Kersley	15	07
John Liphot of Bolton	21	04
George Seddon[76] of dᵒ	16	07
John Smethurst[77] of dᵒ	13	07
John Houseman[78] of dᵒ	20	04
Margᵗ Sharpless of Heaton	23	05
Sarah Sherwood of Congerton	17	05
Elizabeth Nichols of Wiggan	30	05
Alexʳ Jones of Denbyshire	12	10
Margᵗ Waring of Queens County in Ireland	22	04
Elizabeth Ward of Eaton [?] in Lancashire	40	04
William Ward of dᵒ	13	10
Henry Butterfeild of Hallifax	16	08
Rober Maurice of Denbyshire	20	04
Richard Harris of Denby shire	26	04
Tho: Radcliff of Radcliff in Lanc	21	05
Mary Midclare of Macclesfield	24	05
Henry Ascroft of Aughton	20	04
James Birchenough of Wildbore Clough in Cheshire	25	04
John Johnson of Gorsworth in dᵒ	40	04
Mary Clayton of Adlington in dᵒ	24	04
Sarah Hilton of Hazlinton in dᵒ	25	04
William Pickering of Macclesfield	14	07
Henry Turner of Macclesfield	19	04
James Pickering[79] of Macclesfield	20	04
Ann Vavasor of Sporington in Yorkshire	23	05
Ralph Smith of Bolton in Lanc'	15	07
Ralph Kershaw of Longworth	23	04

[74] Kirkby Stephen.
[75] The following items refer to Leyland: Adam, s. of Thomas Somner, taylor, of Leyland, bapt. 12 Oct. 1680. Thomas Sumner and Ellin Whittle of Leyland m. 6 Dec. 1674. Thomas Sumner and Elizabeth Rochett, both of Leyland, m. 23 July 1677. Thomas Somner and Ellin his wife of Leyland Mosside bur. 10 Dec. 1680.
[76] George Seddon, s. of Thomas and Jennet of Bolton, b. 17 Jan., bapt. 23 Jan., 1680-1 at Bolton.
[77] John Smethurst, s. of James and Alice of Bolton, b. 1 Mar., bapt. 6 Mar., 1686-7.
[78] John Houseman s. of James and Mary, bapt. 15 Feb. 1679-80.
[79] The following items refer to Macclesfield: James, son of James Pickering of Macclesfield, bapt. 27 Sept. 1675. James, s. of James Pickering of Macclesfield, bapt. 1 June 1676. James Pickering and Frances Ouldfield, both of Macclesfield, m. 22 June 1673.

Charles Physick of Latham	8 – 14
James Gill of Latham	17 – 05
Wᵐ Physick of Latham	17 – 05
Tho : Physick of dº	11 – 10
Ellen Physick of dº	37 – 04
James Barnes of Hazledine Parish in dº	28 – 04
Will Ollerhead of Tervin in Cheshire	21 – 05
Mary Goare of ormskirk in Lanc	22 – 06
Margery Fairclough of Chorly in dº	14 – 07
Margᵗ Fairclough of dº	16 – 06
Ann Fairlclough [sic] of dº	37 – 04
Wᵐ Fortclough [sic] of dº	12 – 10
Ann Ashley of Boaden in Cheshire	20 – 05
Tho : Robertshaw of Downham in Lancashire	21 – 04
Wᵐ Coverly of Downham in dº	25 – 04
Robert Emett of dº	18 – 05
Tho : Bulcock of dº	22 – 04
Christopher Smith of dº	20 – 04
Will Bulcock of dº	17 – 05
Will Shenock of Downham	16 – 06
Joseph Monk of Clayton in Lanc	20 – 04
Will Hertland of Clerk Hill near Burnley	11 – 11
John Horne of Bishopᵏ of Durham	20 – 04
John Williams of Cryddun in Carnarvanshire	12 – 10
William Pollard of Burnley in Lanc'	21 – 04
Margᵗ Coales of yᵉ Isle of Man	16 – 05
Frances Jackson of City of Chester	17 – 05
Ellen Smith of Sommerset in Lanc'	20 – 06
Ann Waller of Winton in Westmoreland	19 – 04
Joseph Wennington [of] Wheales in Cumberland	20 – 04
Jane Whitehead of Tarleton in Lanc'	17 – 04
John Terroy of London	23 – 04
John Walmsley of Ackrington in Lanc'	20 – 04
Nicholas Whittle [80] of Lealand	22 – 04
Kath Robinson of Hootown in Cheshire	20 – 04
Rober Turner of Tarleton and his daughter	28 : 4 – 05 : 17
Isabel of dº and Son Thomas	20 : ¾ – 05 : 20¼
Richᵈ Snailum [81] of Bretherton	26 – 04
Robert Woods of Bretherton	14 – 06

Account of Servᵗˢ bound to Mʳ Samuell Smith Since 10ᵗʰ of Octoʳ 1700

	Yers Age
William Muddiford of Yorkshire	5 – 27

Servᵗˢ to Mʳ Thomas Presson 23ᵈ Octoʳ 1700

Thomas Hamson of Kilton in Lanc	5 – 22

---

[80] Nicholas, s. of Nicholas Whittle and Alice Parker, a bastard, bapt. 19 Apr. 1676, at Leyland.
[81] Richard Snailem and Anne Porter, both of Bretherton, m. 3 Feb. 1696-7 at Croston.

An Acc[t] of Servants bound to m' Ralph W[m]son 9b. 23. 1699

Eliz.–Ellis of Leedes	aged 20 yeares –	6
Amie Pritchard of Hallywell	aged 23 –	6
James Stewart of Northumberlan'	12 –	10
Mary Howard of Rightington Lanc'	25 –	6
Agnes Sherman of Malstonn [82] Westmorland	17 –	6
Jerom' Taylor of Doncasd' Yorksh'	26 –	5
Jno Lipscom of Sudbery near Bristol	27 –	5
W[m] Hussy of Wellington Somersetsh'	20 –	5
Tho: Williams of Monmouth in Wales	30 –	4
Ann Ellis[83] of Leeds Yorkshire	23 –	6
Elizabeth Waters of Westhoughton Lanc'	22 –	6
J[no] Glave of Hope parish in Flintshire	19 –	5
Tho: Ascome of Padyam [84] in Lancash'	12 –	12
Arthur Dewhurst of Whiston in Lanc'	10 –	12
Tho: Walker of Barnacre in Lanc'	27 –	4
Mary Walker of Barnacre	22 –	4
Tho: Widop of Wadsworth in Yorksh'	17 –	7
Jno Williams of Mosteyn Flintsh'	14 –	8
Hugh Kenardy of Scotland	35 –	5
W[m] Woolfet [85] of Bolton Lanc	15 –	7
J[no] Johnson of London	22 –	5
Tho: Robinson of Richwood Oxfordshr	25 –	4
Ann Hughes of Denbyshire	23 –	6
Daniel Kennion of Berry Lanc	18 –	5
J[no] Murrough of Northumberl'	14 –	10
Josh.' Tunstall of Billing	18 –	6
Ann Penry of Rochdall	18 –	6
Adam Auger of Northumberl'	12 –	11
Charles Mendam of Norridg Citty	19 –	5
J[no] m[tt] Donell [sic] of Scotl[i]	19 –	6
J[no] Alicer of Taunton Somersetsh'	21 –	5
J[no] Pennington of Little Emsell in Yorsh'	25 –	5
Tho: Hudson of Maun in Yorksh'	19 –	5
Rob[t] Southworth of Kinsley Staffordsh'	16 –	7
J[no] Low of Ashton in Lanc	30 –	4
Mary Statham of Lichfield	20 –	6
Daniel Burridg of Shrewsberry	26 –	5
Alexand Blandford of Plimouth Devonsh'	22 –	6
Ellis Scowfield of Rochdall	25 –	5
J[no] Ashworth of Rochdall	30 –	5
Xpr. Tyrer of West-Derby	18 –	6
James Thelwell of Cuerdley Shoomak'	22 –	5
Ann Walker of Manchest'	19 –	6
Grace Edmund [of] Carnarvansh'	20 yeares –	6
Thomas Ewes of Colehill Warwicksh'	20 –	4

[82] Mallerstang.

[83] At St. Peter's Church, Leeds: Ann, child of Samuel Ellis of ye Nether Headrow, b. 5 June, bapt. 18 June, 1673. Samuel Ellis and Elizabeth Threlford of Lower Head-drow m. 6 Apr. 1669.

[84] Padiham.

[85] William Woolfet, s. of Edward and Elizabeth of Little Bolton, b. 27 Dec., bapt. 30 Dec., 1683 at Bolton.

Margtte Brown of Witham Cumberl'	18 – 5
Edw' Gryffin of Carmarthen	25 – 5
James Toppin of Garston	22 – 4
Mary Jones of London	20 – 5
James Wilson of Cardigan	24 – 4
Wm Plumb of Hollinfare	16 – 9
Wm Sedden of Hinley	20 – 5
Eliz : Cotton near Blackburne	18 – 7
Jno Wainwright of Halewood	11 – 11
Sarah Eaton of Budworth	20 – 4
Eliz : Marsh of Budworth	16 – 6
Tho : Mosse of Budworth	16 – 6
Joseph Elwood	19 – 4
Jno Beckett Bricklayer of the Citty of York	30 – 4
Joseph Briggs of Ratchdale	18 – 7
Isaac Harrisson of of [sic] Ditton	13 – 7
Thomas Daw of Birtinwood Lancashire	25 – 5
Jeremiah Cronage of Leeds : Yorkshire	17 – 4

9b. 24   Samuel Sadler of Witt-   ⎧ To m' Lund   ⎫ 23 yeares
         nough   ⎨   ⎬ bound for
         Cheshir' Milwright   ⎩ m' Houghtons friend ⎭ 5 yeares

Febre : 22° 1699
      Thom' Parke of Much Hool in the County of Lanc. aged
      21 Appr to m' Tho : Hayes for Acct. of Thom. Johnson jr
      Ery [sic] 4 yeares
      Jno Sutherland Son of James Sutherland of Elgin in Scotlan'
      aged ab. 15 to ye same fr 7 yeares

Febru : 27. 1699
      Evan Owen of or near Ossestry in Shropshr'
            agd   20 yeares – 4
27 : 1699 Tho : Williams of Carnarvan in Wales   12 yeares – 9

To m' Wm Benn.
March 21. 1699
      Robt Jayes of Tuam County of Galloway in Ireland   4

To Capt Clayton
March 26–1700
      Wm Thompson of London Mason   agd 31 – 4
      who went also in ye ship wth m' Wm Benn

      Bryan Blundell Servants to Henry Williams
            of Cornarvanshire   9 – 16
      John Thomas [of] Cornarvanshire   6 – 19
November 7th 1700 Servts to Mr John Henry of Maryland
      John Key of Yorkeshire   4 – 25
      William Jackson of Lancashire   4½ – 27

Samuel Simpcock to John Cocke   6 – 24

8b. y^e : 15. 1700

            Ann Buckley of Salford to m' Robt Moon 6 yeares aged 22
        16 Henry Williams of Flintshire   9 yeares ag^d 15
8^br 21°   Benedictus Chestain of Mancheste   6   18
            Jane Buckley of Salford   6   19
            Thomas Bradbury Weston   5   24
            Mary Pye Knowsley   5   30

Serv^ts with John Charters Octo^r 16– 1700
            francis Fanco' [of] Norrmondy   4   25
            John Wilson [of] Denbishire   4   21
            John Rowlands [of] Denbishire   4   24
            Henry Griffin [of] Denbishire   4   20

17 October 1700 Serv^ts to Mr Basnett
            Johh Nutter of Yorkshire   8 – 14

Servants bound to Mr Augustine Woodward to Virginia the 12^d day of Octo^r 1700 in the Virginia Merch^t.

	Y^s old	Yeares
Elizabeth Leafield of Lancashire	20 –	7
Mary Masson of Cheshire	20 –	5
Margarett Vpton of Cheshire	18 –	4
Anne Wharton of Cheshire	17 –	5
John Coloct of Nottinghamshire	11 –	11
Martha Kilshaw of Cheshire	18 –	4
Elizabeth Naylor of the City of Chester	18 –	5
Jeremiah Boucker of the Citty of London	20 –	4
Thomas Pope of the Citty of London	20 –	4
Elizabeth Hughes of Flintshire in Wales	20 –	7
John Griffith of Denbishire in Wales	12 –	9
Richd Owens of Cardiganshire in Wales	18 –	7
Mary Williams of Anglesie in Wales	11 –	11
Henry Roberts of Flintshire	21 –	7
John Thomas of Flintshire	11 –	11
John Robert of Flintshire	12 –	10
Thomas Roberts of Flintshire	14 –	8
Evan Owens of Carnarvanshire aged	11 –	11
William Robinson of Northumberland	16 –	7
William Stafford of Cheshire	17 –	6
John Spooner of Derbyshire	32 –	4
John Balie of Lancashire	20 –	4
Kath: Thomas of Wales	22 –	5
Evan Evans of Wales	25 –	4

Servants bound to Mr William Part to Virginia the Nineteenth day of November in the Elizabeth & Judeth

            John Mathews of Whitehaven   17 – 5
            John Medley of Yorkshire   19 – 7

Nicholas Butterworth of Yorkshr^e	19	7
Henry Walbanck of d°	24	5
Robt Ratt[ ] D°	22	5
William Boy D°	22	5
Rab^m. [sic] Shaftin	21	5

Servants bound on board Mr Jonathan Leivsay

Edm^d Knowles of Boulton aged	15	7

xb 16 1700   Servants bound to Mr Henry Browne
John Oglebie [of] Edenboraugh, Aged 19 Yeares,
    According to the Custome
John Horsbell of the Same Aged 16 Yeares D°

William Maddock of Chester	21	5
Charles Edw^ds of Wales	12	12
John Loyd of d°	11	13
Wm Edwards d°	10	14
Tho : Mathews d°	9	15
Michal Hughes d°	15	7
Tho Owens d°	17	7
Edwd Jones d°	15	9
Sam. W^mso' d°	14	10
Jo^seh Griffith d°	17	7

Servants bound To m' Daniell Murphy To Virginia in the Shill [sic]
John Baptist the Twelfth of December 1700

Elizabeth Thompson of Chester	28	5
Isabella Sellors of Liverpoole	24	7
John Mills of Lansh	12	9
John Barroms of Kent	16	5
Thomas Duglas of Northumberland	29	4
James Johnson of Lanc'	21	4
Wm Hicks of Elesmore	22	4
Richard Style of Cheshire	19	4
Timothy Hicks of Elesmore	16	4
Samuell Breerely of Lanc	15	7
Edward evans of denbishire	12	7
Jonie Fletcher of Staffordshire	22	4
Ellen Foster of Namtwich Aged	27	4
John Morgan of Wales	13	7
Margrett Hebbett of Cheshire	21	4
Sarah Clough of Holywell	17	6
Elizabeth Rogers of Cheshire Aged	18	6
Hester Jones of Cheshire	18	6
Howell Jones of Cheshire	23	4

An Account of Servants bound to Mr Thomas Leskonby for Virginia on
board the Shipp Globe the Twenty Third day of January 1700

Alexander Harginson of Newcastle aged	5	8
John Gage of the Citty of London	22	4
Daniell Steward of the Citty of London	15	8

	Mary Booth of Lancashire	22 –	4
	Anne Birch of Lancashire	20 –	4
	Richard Rowlands of Westmoreland	24 –	4
	Elizabeth Pamwitt of Cumberland	22 –	5
	Henry Justice of Chester	21 –	5
	Samuell Gurdain of Lanc	28 –	4
	Thomas Fenne of Lancashire	24 –	4
	Anne Humphrys of Herefordshire	22 –	5
	Robert Whitacre of Lancashire	19 –	4
	Robert Siddall of Whithington neare Manchester	23 –	4
R : :	Edwd Fitchgerrard of London aged 30 Yeares		4

Servants bound to Mr Henry Smith for Virginia on board the Anne & Sarah the Twenty Third day of January 1700.

	William Morris of Lancashire	36 –	4
	Mary Morris of the same vx^r	30 –	4
	Richard Simons of Liverpoole	21 –	4
	Mary Boucker of Lancashire	22 –	4
	Elizabeth Lunt of Lancashire	23 –	4
	Richard Abraham of Lanc'	20 –	5
	James Hall of Northumberland	26 –	5
	James Wilson of Northamptonshire	20 –	5
	John Bowker of Lancashire	24 –	4
	Abraham Bowker D^o	18 –	4
	William Briggs of Lanc'	22 –	4

Servants bound to Virginia on board of the Robert and Elizabeth to M' Ralph Williamson 27th January 1700

	Elizabeth Naylor of Exiter	26 –	4
	Henry Scoffield of Lanc^r	40 –	4
	Andrew Bird of Shropshire	18 –	4
	John Whitacre of Lanc^r	30 –	4
	Nathaniell Lidnescey of Hampshire	26 –	4
	Peter Gowen of Yorkshire	20 –	4
	Mary Mills of Lancashire	23 –	5
	Thomas Thornley of Cheshire	16 –	7
	Owen Jones of Anglisie	20 –	4
	Barbury Lensey of Yorkshire	20 –	4
	John Frankland of Middlesex	21 –	5
	Elizabeth Briggs of Hull	19 –	4
	Richard Radley of Manchester	37 –	4
	Thomas Most of Lanc'	19 –	4
	James Maddock of Lanc'	30 –	4
	Christopher Marsden of Lanc'	20 –	5
	Samuell Browne of Whiston in Lanc'	16 –	7
	Susan Lea of Cheshire	29 –	4
	Anne Edward of Wales	25 –	5
	Elizabeth Camell of Lanc^r	16 –	8
	Elizabeth Davies of Shrowsbury	24 –	5
Run away	Diana Molyneux of Chester	20 –	5
	Sarah Bridg of Cheshire	25 –	5
	James Cartwright of Shropshire Bridgnorth	30 –	5

Run away	Thomas Pearson of Newcastle	21 – 4
	Daniell Williams of Herefordshire	24 – 4
	Robt Goodwin of Lanc^r	22 – 4
	John Harrison of Liverpoole	21 – 4
	Thomas Hardman of Lanc^r	30 – 4
	Evan Evans of Mountgomeryshire	40 – 5
	Margarett Evans of d^o	30 – 5
	William Wright of Rudlandshire	30 – 4
	Elizabeth Wright D^o	30 – 5
	Rachell Pattison [of] Cheshire	19 – 5
	Martha Marchie	19 – 5
	Jonathan Plowman of Yorkshire	12 – 10
	Peter Harrison of Lanc'	24 – 4
	paid by Mr Marsden	
	Wm Pers of Lancashire	21 – 4
	Richd Rustin of Chalk in Weltshire Tayl'	21 – 4
	J^n Heal of Cirencest' in Glowstershir Tay^l	21 – 4
	J^{no} Gath of Carlisle 5 year	20 – 5

Servants bound to M' William Everard the Eleaventh day of February 1700: on board of the Shipp the Lambe of Liverpoole

	Richard Lewis of Mereonithshire	11 – 7
	William Davies of Dorsetshire aged	24 – 4
	Thomas Jones of Denbishire	29 – 4
	William Davies of Denbishire	21 – 4
	Joseph Gibson of Travellin in Wales	16 – 7
	Thomas Worrall of Nantwich	20 – 4
	Thomas Davis of Denbishire	21 – 5
	Robert Morris of Shropshire	22 – 4
	Robert Hughes of Carnarvanshire	15 – 9
	John Hodgkinson of Liverpoole aged	9 – 11
	Randle Carters of Cheshire	20 – 6
	James Towning of Lodg.[86]	17 – 5
	Christopher Parkinson [87] of Chipping	17 – 5
	John Peares of Flintshire	18 – 7
	Randle Fidians of Cheshire	22 – 4
	John Dod of Denbyshire	30 – 4
	David Jones of Denbishire	19 – 7
	Griffith Hughes of Wales	18 – 5
	Thomas Briscoe of Chester	22 – 4
Run	David Williams of Mountgomeryshire	35 – 4

rememb. Hugh Topping of Waringh'

Servants bound to to [sic] M' John Hughes the Tenth day of February 1700

	Mary Owery of Denbishire aged	15 – 8
	Margarett Nicholls of Flintshire	26 – 5

[86] Lodge, Yorks, or The Lodge, Shropshire (?)
[87] The following items refer to Chipping: Christopher, s. of Robert Parkinson of Chepin, bapt. 5 Mar. 1681-2. Robert, s. of John Perkinson of Cock hill, bapt. 12 May 1681. Robert, s. of Richard Perkinson of Chippin, bapt. 26 Sept. 1655.

Serv^ts to M' John Charters on board the Lambe of Liverpoole 11th Feb^ry 1700

Robert Oglebie of Lanc'	17 –	4
John Brittin of Lancashire	22 –	4

Serv^ts bound to M' Tho: Heyes To Antego this 8 day of March 1700

Paid 1° Apr 1701 { John Low of Lanc' Aged ...... 16 – 6
William Lealand of Boulton in Lanc ...... 13 – 7

Nov 1° 1701 Serv^ts to Mr Tho: Williamson

Joshua Rycroft of Cheshire Aged ...... 12 – 8

Nov: 1° 1701 Servants bound to M' William Part

Ralph Cockett of Dunyan [88] Aged	15 –	7
Elizabeth Stansel [A]ged 21 Yeares	21 –	4
Robert Jackson of Lanc' A[ged]	15 –	7
Ellen Roson of Lanc' Aged	20 –	4
Mary Harefoote of Ormshire	19 –	4

November 8th 1701

Serv^ts bound to Mr John Gore

Ship7Serving men p^d per J^n: Cockshutt

Elizabeth Wright of Cheshire Aged ab^t [89]	21 –	5
Joseph Tagg of d°	20 –	5
Michaell Aldridg of Yorkeshire	40 –	4
Richard Pearson of Northampton	26 –	5
Easter Miers of Lanc^r	20 –	5
Mary Oragehead of Cheshire	20 –	5
Abigall Bradshaw of d°	27 –	5

No: Eighth: Servants bound to Mr Samuell Medgley

Eliz Oakes [of] Cheshire	18 –	4
p' Alice Slator d°	20 –	4
Jane Robinson [of] Lancaster	20 –	4

25 Octo^br 1701 Tho Buttler Son of Wm Buttler to Ganther Carefoote for 7 Yeares

Serv^ts to M' Edwd Tarleton 21 of November 1701

Walter Richards of Herefordshire ...... 33 – 4

Serv^ts to Mr Basnett

Eliz Voughan of the Citty of London ...... 20 – 7

4° Decem^r 1701. Serv^ts to Mr John Greene

William Peares of Carnarvanshire ...... 12 – 9

4 Decem^r 1701 Servants bound to William Gurdon

	aged	
James Smallwood [of] Cheshire Aged	27 –	4
Ann Goodwin d°	22 –	4
9 Richd Dinsdall of Wenswide in Yorkshire	32 –	4

[88] Dunham (?)
[89] This and the six items following it are crossed out in the original.

Serv^{ts} to M' Nehemiah Jones   4 december 1701
          Joseph Gregg Apprentice of Ashton   22 – 5

Servants bound to m' Michael Wentworth   28th 9b 1701
          Thomas Greene of Yorkshire aged between 27 yrs for 6
          yeares
          Joshua Thompson of Yorkshire aged about 20 yeares for 6
          yeares

Jan 3 1701   John Medecine App to m' Andrew Clark for 9 yeares, y^e
             s^d John Medecine aged about 13 yeares

Janu' 5 1701 Serv^{ts} to m' Henry Brown
             John Patience of Wiltshire husband' aged about 34 yeares

             James Hamer of Acper in Lancashire near Wigan is sus-
             pected to go abroad & I am Oblig^d to Stop him.

Serv^{ts} bound to John Ball
                                                          Y
             John Whitehead of Wrixen in Lanc^r Aged   15 – 9
Servants bound to Thurstan Brachall
             Mary Allam of Warrington   20 – 5

12th February 1701
             Serv^{ts} bound to Mr Augustine Woodward
                                                          Age   time
             Wm Beniford of Cheshire   15 – 9
             John Askie of Cheshire   14 – 9
             Sarah Heanes of London Spinst'   21 – 5
21 Feb   Melicent Astly aged 12 years   12 – 7
             Mary Taylor of Staffordshire   18 – 5
             Eliz: Thomas of Wrexam   30 – 5
             Eliz: Morris of Leverp^l Spinstr   25 – 4
24 Jan'   Mary Jones of Brecknockllin   17 – 5
             James Feshel of Cheshire   30 – 4
             Margtte Hughes of Whitby in Cheshire   13 – 9
             Ann Hardgrace of Lancashir   22 – 4
             Wm Brindley of London Shoomakr   25 – 4
             Hannah Yales of Chester Spins'   20 – 5
March 5 1701 Margarette Welsly of Speak   19 – 6

             To m' Edw' Smalley
Feb 26   Ann Pugh of Much Woolton   20 – 4

Feb 4   Tho: Chorter of Manchest to Adam Oldfiel 2 : [sic] – 5

Servants to m' Wm Benn M^r of ye Eliz & Ann to Virgin'
Feb^r 19   J^no Howard of Witherilach Lancashir   28 – 5
Feb 24   William Gedlin of Lancashir   18 – 5

June 29 1702 Servants to m' Thomas Jameson of Maryland
     Edwd Jaspers of Namptwich in Cheshire Tayl^r 21 – 4
July 1 Alexand^r Tyror to m' Thos Jameson   19 – 9
July 1 William Hoyl of Hallifax in Yorkshire 12 – 11
July 3 Richard Anderton of Knowesley   13 – 9

July 6 Wm Edge of Manchest^r Servt to Wm Evrard 17 – 7
  14 Jane Chadwick of Clievland near Yorkshire 24 – 5

To m' Smalwood & m' Everard
Aprel 19th 1702

                  Yeares
    Abraham Su[   ] of Leeds Yorkshire to m'
    Smalwood   aged 15 – 9
June 19 1702 Moses Rithwell of Chester   16 – 7
June 27 Jno Marshall [of] Southampton   15 – 8
July 6 Ann Heward [90] of Berry Lancashire 20 – 7
 6 Jane Knight of Congleton   30 – 7
 6 Anna Crosfield of Cartmell Lancar 18 – 7

Aug. 14 1702 Luke Perrey to m' [*blank*]
    to m' Stephen H [*blotted*]
8b. 6 1702 John Earthead of Brinly in Lancashire 18 – 7
8b ye 10 1702 James Burl of Westmoreland Ag' 27 – 4

                 ag' time
8b. 15 1702 Henry Wilson Servant to m' Wm Peters 14 – 7

Servants to m' Nehem. Jones
Janu' first Thom' Hart of Ashton   17 – 7
    Mary Morris of Ashto   18 – 6
    J^{no} Tyrr of Liverpoole   18 – 6

9b 17th 1702 Richard Peling Son of Georg Peling late of ye Citty of
    Chester Shoomaker aged about 16 Yeares hath bound
    himselfe a Serv to Barbadoes or any other of ye Charyb-
    bee Island for 7 yeares, after his Arrival at Barbadoes or
    one of ye s^d Islands

                   age yrs
xb. 7. 1702 Mary Fish of Whittle in ye Woods Lancas App^r
    to m' Gilb: Eden Or his Assigns to Virg. or
    Maryland [91]   29 – 5

xb. 8. 1702 Jane Morgan serv^t: to m' J^{no} Lancast 14 –

                  Age year
xb. 16. 1702 Richard Hatton of Tarbook to sd Andr' Clarke
    of Belfast   29 4

---

[90] At Bury: "An," dau. of Roger Hewood, b. 20 Nov., bapt. 10 Dec., 1682. Roger Hayward of Moorside d. 22 Mar., bur. 23 Mar., 1698.
[91] This entry crossed out in the original record. *Vide infra* for duplicate entry.

xb^r 21   Wm Philips of Cork in Ireland to m' : J^{no} Lancst 48   4

xb. 26 1702   J^{no} Fooles of Cabin in Lancast husbndm'   25   4

Jan : 8. 1702 Roger Preswicke of Manchr Taylor to Randle
            Platt   20   4

Jan : 9 : 1702 Ralph Bate of Croft hus to Capt. Henry Brown   22 :   5

Jan 13 1702 Timothy Dickinson of Stockport Chap'   35 :   4

Jan. 16 1702 Alice Steel of Knutsford in Cheshire   21 :   4

Jan. 20 : 1702 Robt Buckley of Cronton   15 :   9

    20 :   Ann Steed of Sephton   25 :   5

    20 :   Mary Woods [92] of Bolton   23 :   5

To Tho W^mson

March 5th 1702
            Richard Forber of Whiston   17 :   6

To m' Ralph W^mson

March 17 1702
            Kather' Williams of Abborguelley [93] in Wales   18 :   6

    17   Wm Parrey of Ridgland [94] in Wales   18 :   6

To m Wm Robinson

March 17 : 1702
            J^{no} Mercer Son of J^{no} Merce' of Eurton Shoo-
            make'   15 :   6

An Acc^t : of Serv^{ts} : in ye Tabitha and Priscill Capt Wm Tarleton
Comand^r

                                           Age   Year

28 : Ja' 1702 Jno Harrison of Liverpoole Assign^d to m' James
            Tildesley   24   4

Feb 3   Jno Humphrey of Denbyshire to m' Geo' : Tyrer
            & Assign^d to m' Tildesly   12 :   9

7 xb.   Mary Fish of Whittle in ye Woods in Lancaste'
            Spins^t to m'. Eden Ap. to m'. Tildesley   29 –   5

18 xb.   Richd Webb son of Edw'. Webb of London In-
            keep, to m' Geo : Tyrer assign^d to m' Tildesly   16 :   7

9 Ja'   Jane Granth' of Olringham in Cheshire   23 :   4

1 Jan'   Ann Tool of Fingall in Ireland Spinst^r to m' W^m
            Tarleton & by him assign^d to m' James Til-
            desley   21 :   4

6 : Feb   James Hatton of Boughton in Cheshir   14 :   7

29. Jan'   Eliz : Valentine of Liverpoole   21 :   5

March 20 : 1702
            Ellen Hughes of Denbishire to Daniel Faurell Carpen^t of y^e
            Brittania   21 :   5

---

[92] Mary Wood, dau. of Samuel and Dorothy of Breightmet, b. 27 Jan., bapt. 29 Jan., 1682–3, at Bolton.

[93] Abergele.

[94] Raglan (?)

An Acc[t] of Serv' Bound to m': J[no] Charters Anno 1702

		Age	Yeares
January 20.	James Low of Prescott	15 :	4
28.	Mary Robinson of Thornton of Dalamores[95] in Cheshire Spinst	20 :	4
Feb 20 :	Eliz : Wright of Liverpoole Spinst[r]	15 :	4
17 :	Jinnet Roy[l] of Preston in Lancash' Spins[t]	19 :	4
Jan 18 :	Eliz : Dixon of ye Town of Lancs[r] Spins[t]	20 :	4
18 :	Mary Fletcher[96] of Macclesfield in Cheshire Spinst	16 :	4
29 :	James Brown of Carleton in Cumberland	21 :	4
March 10	James Aldorson of Helig in sneidale in y[e] County of York	22 :	4
10	J[n] Hunter of Askrigg in Yorkshire	18 :	4
Apr[l] 9. 1703	Eliz : Hughes of Wrexam	21 :	5
9 :	Marg[tt] Gaylen of Ruthin	36 :	5

To m' : Samuel Sanford

Feb. 15. 1702	Peter Wilson of Carlisle	12 :	9
25	Thom' Rawson of Wrexam in Wales	14 :	6
March 27	W[m] Heyes	16 :	7

To m' Joseph Briggs
Janu' 19. 1702

	Thom' : Elleson of Preston on y[e] Hill in Cheshire	12 :	9
20 :	Eliz : Johnson of Macklesfield in Cheshire	25 :	4
12 :	Ezekiel Holms of Frodsham	15 :	7
6 :	W[m] Hamlet of Wavetree	10 :	11

To m' : J[no] Gore

Ap' 2. 1703	J[no] Ashton of Whiston	20 :	5
	Anne Steed of Jure Lan	21 :	5
	Rich[d] Jakeman of Skipton brawn Yorksh	22 :	4
	Mary Woods of Boltou	22 :	5
	Rob[t] Buckley near Preston	13 :	9
March 17	Rich[d] Ronell of Livrpoole	20 :	4
3	[blank] Penkell	20 :	5
Feb. 27	Peter Penkell Pieer [last two words crossed out]	12 :	11

To m'. Richard Lathom

		age	year
April 6. 1703	Rich[d] Ingam[97] of Wood Plumpton in Lanc	30 :	4
Ap'. 10. 1703	John Jackson son of Rich[d] of Preston Inkeep[r]	—	4

To m' Thos Leavins

April 7	W[m] Isherwood of Bolton Lancast	16 :	7

April 12. 1703	to m' J[no] Gore John Pelton of [blank] in Lancashire	13 :	9

[95] Thornton-le-More or, as it was probably called at that time, Thornton de la More.
[96] Mary, dau. of Alexander Fletcher of Macclesfield, bapt. 1 May 1687 at Macclesfield.
[97] Richard Ingham and Ellin Porter, both of Wood Plumpton, m. 18 Sept. 1692.

15. 1703 Easter Deakin of Toxteth Park in Lancashire   22 : 5
21: 1703 James Johnson   18 : 7
26: 1703 Ann Linacre of Livrpoole   38 : 4

Servants bound to m' Thomas Hughes
xb. 17. 1702 Edwd Tatlocke of Childwall in Lancashire   22⁻: 5
March 23. 1702/3
     Kath' Prier of Carmarthenshire   21 : 5
Ap'. 1. 1703   Pemberton Proudlow of Sandwich in Cheshire   15 : 9
     Steph' Christian   30 : 4
Ap'. 20 : 1703 J^no Evans of Anglesy in Roskallin[98] Parish   12 : 9

To m' Henry Brown
April 26. 1703 J^no Poston Off Shrewsberrey   17 : 5

April 26. 1703 Ruth Lingard to m' Joseph Briggs   18 : 4

April 26. 1703 Evan Jones of Carnarvansh to m' J^n Charters   30   4

April 29. 1703 Thom' Wharton of Eurton to m' Richd Wright
     in ye Brittan to Virgin'   19 : 5

Servants bound to M' Nathn^l Hughes 2 Augt 1702
     Dorathy Tipping of Garston Lancasr   21 : 4
16. April 93 [sic]   Mary Adrick of Barton Lanc   21 : 4
17. Feb. 1702 Mary Moor of Aughton Lan'   25 : 4
28. 8b. 1702   Eliz : Sharp of Pelton Lanc   18 : 4
23. 8b. 1702   Margar^tt Taylor of Ratclffe Lancast   18 : 5
16 Feb. 1702 Ellen Owen of Farnith Lanc'   20 : 4
7 March 1702 Georg Burgesse of Preston   22 : 4
20 Janu' 1702 Henry Lea of Pickdell   14 : 6
     mem   there is one & half more Owing for.

---

                                  yeares
Octob 9 1703 Wm Watson[99] Son of Saml Watson late of Macclesf^d }
     in Cheshire gent Servt to m' Bryan Brundell   }   4

An Acc^t of Servants bound to m J^no Smalwood to go in ye Lamb
                               age   years
Aug^st 13 1703 Philip Stockton of Clayton Parish Lanc   14 : 7
    14   James Dawson of Lealand   14 : 8
7b   17   Sarah Johnson [of] Pontefract in Yorksh'   22 : 5
    20   Tho : Slater of Manches^t   20 : 5
    30   Alice Chadwyck of Brindle Lancasr'   20 : 5
    13   Ellen Hodgson of Thornton   : 5

---

[98] Rhoscolyn.
[99] "Gulielmus Watson filius Samuelis Watson generosi et Sarae vxoris Eius natus fuit Primo Die Martij Baptizatusq in Capella Parochiali de Macclesfeild Decimo Tertio die Die Ejusdem mensis Annoque domi 1672–3." From the Church Registers of Macclesfield. This Latin entry, which is in a large and elaborate hand, covering half a page, in contrast to the carelessly written and abbreviated form used in other entries, shows the social importance of the family.

	9	Henry Lloy^d of Conway in Wales	15 : 8
8b	1	Jno Living of Manchest'	
	4	Mary Platt of Preston on ye Hill Chesh	23 : 4
	8	Eliz Lewis of Foodild Parish Cheshir	23 : 5
		Mary Stewart of London	25 : 7
		[ ] of Cheshire	

To m' Jno Birch

9b. 1 1703   Thom Prestidg of Vardy Green, near Manches'   15 : 7

To m Peter Man

Janu : 25th 1703   Mary Fletcher of Whiston Spinst aged   21 : 5

To m' J^{no} Laurill

Janr 12 1703	Kath' Hughes of Arlslie in the County of Salip Spinst	22 : 4
ead die	Margtte Dickinson of Wavertree Spinst	22 : 4
Feb 7 1703	Alice Bertinsh' of Manch' Spinst	21 : 4
Fbr ead die	Hannah Hairclipe of Hallifax in ye County of York Widow	27 : 4
Feb. 4. 1703	William Yates of Prescott husbandm'	18 : 4
2. 1703	Ellen Whitlisse of Hinley Spinst. to m Richd Gildart but Assign' to Capt Lancst'	15 : 7
Febr. 9 1703	Saml Hartless of Sanbych in Cheshire to m' : Thom' Williamson but assigned to m' Jⁿ Lancast'	

To m' Peter Hall

March 31. 1704 William Strickland Appr. to m' Peter Hall   14 : 10

To m' : Nathaniel Hughes to go in y^e : great Eliz :

April 5	Eliz : Cooper of Hanforth Spinst : in Cheshire	24 : 4
5	Ann Lingard of M^{cc}lesfield in Cheshire	24 : 4
5	Mary Williams of Holywell Spinst	16 : 5
5	Mary Lawrence of Liverpoole Spr	24 : 4
5	Ann Bowland of Chester Spr	20 : 4
22	Hanna Croswell of Livrp Spr	22 : 4
M' 5	Thomas Hughes of Walton [ ]withems	15 : 5

To m' William Par^t

		age	years
July 15. 1704	Marth' Wilson of Macclesfield in Cheshire Spinst	21 :	5
Augt 1. 1704	Jane Richson of Workington in Cumberland Spinst	25 :	5
Augt 10 : 1704	Jane Miller of Macclesfield in Chestr Spinst	22 :	5
10 : 1704	Ralph Langley of Tamouth[100] in Warwyckshire	16 :	4
10 : 1704	Elizabeth Meakin of Dublin Spins^t	16 :	5
19 : 1704	Jane Clements of Dublin Spinst	21 :	4
7b 11 : 1704	Elizabeth Butler daughter to Eliz : Watkinson } of York Widow p her Mother Consent }	8 :	12
11. 1704	Eliz : Watkinson herself	27 :	4

[100] Tanworth.

7b. 13 : 1704 To [   ] Blundell Esq ; & sent to his Broth.'
m.' Richd Blundell in Virgin.' and hee went in
ye Ship wth Wm Part. J^{no} Blundell of Crosbie
Parva   20 : 7

8b. 17 : 1704 Jonath' Tapley of Norley in Cheshire Taylor to
m' Low   22 : 5
To m : Joseph Parr.

9b. 16.   Eliz : Actin of Tunbridg Spinstr (in Kent   18 : 4

To m' : J^{no} Lancst'
16 : 9b. 1704 Richard Berrey of Dalton in Lancashire   16 : 7

---

20 : 9b. 1704   To m' : Thom' : Leekenber
Thom : Dickinson of or near Leeds in Yorkshire 15 : 6

---

to m' J^{no} Bamster

	age	year
Decemb. 18. 1704 Ann Wainwright of Farnworth	20 :	5

To m' : Ezekiel Parr
Decemb^r 20. 1704 Mary Woolley of Bishops Castle in Shropshire 26 : 4
ead die   Kath' Woodier of Rigat in Surrey   24 : 4

To m' Wm Williamson for acc^t of m'. Johnson
xb. 27. 1704 Mary Mills of Leeke[101] in Shropshire   16 : 4
ead Die   Grace Robinson of Heptonstall in Yorkshire   21 : 4

To Ald^m : John Cockshutte
xb. 28. 1704 Hannah Bridg of Manchester Spinster   20 : 4
30 :   Kath Arch-Deacon of Bramhall town in ye County
of Kilkenny In Ireland Sp.   19 : 4

To Ald^m : Richd Houghton
xb. 30. 1704 J^{no} Bonns of Oustan in ye County of Lincoln Taylor

---

To m' : Thomas Williamson   age
Janu : 5. 1704 Roger Finch of Standish House[102] Carpenter   45 : 4
ead die   Wm Finch of ye same and son to Roger Finch 16 : 7

To m^r : Randle Platt.
Thomas Taylor of Liverpoole   14 : 7

---

[101] Lake.
[102] Is this Standish Hall in the parish of Standish ?

To m' J^{no} Wright

		age	time
April 27. 1705	J^{no} Aspinwall son of Henry Aspinwall of Ashton in ye County of Lancast to S : xprnos[103] or any other of ye Char'ybbee Islands	17	4

To m' : Edward Rochdale

Ap. 27. 1705	Eliz : Parker Daughter of Thomas Parker late Bolton in Yorkshire	20 – 5	
May 1. 1705	Hannah Hewitte of Heplinsdale in Yorkshire spinster	21 – 4	
ead die	Ann Booth[104] of Bradford in Yorkshire spinster	16 – 4	
ead die	Mary Heywood of Great Newton in Staffordshire	18 – 5	
May 22. 1705	Ellen Holme[105] of Manchester in ye County of Lanc Spinst	19 – 4	
June 1 : 1705	Mary Cooper of Prescott in ye County of Lanc Spinst	17 – 6	
5 :	Jane Stewart of ye City of London Spins^t	14 : 6	
14	Ellen Croston of Westhoughton in ye County of Lanc Spins^t	17 – 5	
18 :	Isabel Jones of Rigland[106] in Wales Spinst^r	25 : 4	
20 :	Roger Son of Roger Prestidge of Manchs^t in ye County of Lanc	15 : 7	
21 :	Thomas Hough of Middle Hilton[107] in ye County of Lanc	14 – 7	
27 :	Kath' : Langdon of Whittle in ye County of Lanc	21 – 5	
July 3 :	Ann Brown of Leland in Lancashire	21 – 5	
3 :	Mary Heap of Blackbourne in Lancashire	21 – 5	

To m' : Joseph Preem

7b. 11	Mary Thornton of ye Parish of Stoke in Cheshire Spins'	17 – 6	
7b. 11	James Brown of Sheilds in Northumberland	17 – 6	
7b. 8	Joannah Meredith of Much-wenlock in Shropshire Spn	21 – 5	
7b. 8	J^{no} Hughes of Langadwin in Montgomeryshire in Wales	14 – 7	

To m' : Henry Smith to ye Charybbee Islands Virgin' or Maryland.

9b. 3. 1705	Thomas Mere of Hulton in ye County of Lancas^r husbandm'	5 –16	

To m' : Edward Tarleton j^r

9b. 27. 1705	Wm Smethurst at Hilton[108] of Middleton in ye County of Lancas^t & Son of Andrew Hilton Husbandm	14– 7	

---

[103] St. Christopher.

[104] At Bradford : Ann, dau. of James Booth of Heaton, bapt. 29 Dec. 1689. Ann, dau. of James Booth of Shipley, bapt. 30 Dec. 1689. James Booth and Ann Pollard m. 7 Feb. 1688-9.

[105] Ellen, dau. of John Hulme, Shrewfold, bapt. 26 Dec. 1684 at Didsbury, in the parish of Manchester.

[106] Raglan.

[107] Middle Hulton.

[108] Andrew Hilton of Middleton had eleven children b, betw. 1668 and 1689, when there is a break in the records until 1695. He was bur. 25 Feb. 1696-7. This emigrant was b. abt. 1691. He may have been a son, legitimate or illegitimate, of the above. Andrew, son of William Hilton, bapt. 6 Aug. 1643 at Middleton.

9b. 29. 1705 Jane ye Daughter of Henry Ellison of West Derby husban' 17– 5

xb. 8. 1705 To M': J^{no} Marsden Edwd Ashton of Winwyck Parish 21– 4

xb. 10. 1705 To M' Wm Tarleton Thomas Whalley of Middleton 15– 7

To Thomas Fawsette

xb. 6. 1705 Lawrence Cockshutte of Ecclesell in Lancashire Fustian Weaver 20– 5

To m' Henry Schofield in Potomock in Maryland **Age Years**

9b. 21. 1705 Jno Lucas of Eccles in Lancash' Webster 17 : 5

28 Thom': Hayes of Huddersfield in Yorkshire Chandl^r 30 : 4

To m' J^{no} Smalwood

9b. 9. 1705 J^n Millard in Wedgberry[109] in Staffordshr Nailr 14 : 7

8 : George Lord of Tatnell[110] in Cheshire White Cooper 30 : 4

6 : J^{no} Bradburd of Bradley near Frodsh' in Chesh' 22 : 5

7b. 3 J^{no} Walmesley of Lievsay in Lancast' husband' 13 : 7

was returnd' 3 Sam̄l Berrey of Aston in Cheshire Husband 13 : 7

18 Francis Vandery of Colchestr' in Essex husb' 18 : 6

18 J^{no} Bricknell of Colches' hus' 20 : 6

18 J^{no} Bow of Colches^t husb' 19 : 6

3 Thom': Chaddock of Pendleton Pole husband 12 : 7

Jan^r 4 To m'. J^{no} Marsden, but m': Smalwood pays for them. Jonathan Heendrey of Eccls Parish } 14 – 9

1705 Memo. That when Mr Thomas Preeson went in ye ship called ye Augustine but now called ye Thomas and Elizabeth, hee ow^d me for drawing the 4 Lad Indentures ; and three shillings six pence besides.

To m'. J^{no} Wright

Jan'. 4. 1705 Wm Roberts of Beau mauris Shoomaker p^d 21 – 4

To m'. Matthias Gibson

Jan'. 4. 1705 J^{no} Taylor of Bedford in ye County of Lancst Agd. p^d 16 – 5

To m'. J^n Crane 22^d 9^b 1705

James Woods of Derby in Derbyshire aged — to be allowed on Acc^t 12 – 9

To m'. Ralph W^{m}son Jan 4. 1705

Ellen Roberts near Holywell Spins^t 19 – 4

Ann Whitacre near Clitherou 21 – 4

Eliz: Dene [of] Great Sankey 27 – 4

---

[109] Wednesbury(?).
[110] Tattenhall.

Jan[r] 19. 1705 John Hougland of Kelson[111] in Cheshire to m[r] J[no]
   Periesel for Virgin or y[e] Charybben   16 : 5

     To m'. Hugh Patten   Age Years
Janu' 22[d] 1705 Jacob Jackim of Haughton in y[e] County of Chester 15 – 8
Jan'. 22. 1706 Adam Mosley of Mackelesfield Forrist in Cheshire 15 – 8

    To M[r] John Percivall Febr 2 : 1705
Febuy y[e] 21[t] Rob[t] Harrison[112] of Bretherton in Lanc aged about Fifteene
  yeares to serve in y[e] : Plantations for Seaven Yeares

   Feb : 2 : 1705
   To M[r] Thomas Amery Ellen Low of Hay near Wigan aged
   about sixteene yeares to serve in Virginea or Maryland
   seaven Yeares p[d]
March 6 1705/6 Margtt Cholmondeley of Coat Cales in Lansh' p[d] ag[d] 20 7
   yeares

    Feb : y[e] 5 : 1705
   To M[r] William Oliver, Elizabeth Brookes of Bridgwater in
   Somersetshire aged about Thirty Yeares to serve in Vir-
   ginea or Maryland for Fowr Yeares p[d]

    Ditto Die
   To W[m] Oliver Sarah Needham of Buxton in Darbishire aged
   about 19 Yeares to Serve in Virginea or Maryland for 4
   Yeares.

    To M[r] Lancaster

		Age	Time of Service Yeares
Feb.	Elizab Stanley of Leverpoole Spinst aged	26	– 7
1705	Mary Winstanley[113] of Upholland in y[e] : Co : Lanc'	17	– 5
	Elizabeth Yeoman of Anglesey in Wales	20	– 5
	Alice Crompton of Freckeleton in Lanc'	25	– 5
	Elizabeth Fauster of Samsberry[114] in Lanc'	21	– 5
	Mary Greenhalgh of Chorley in Lanc'	15	– 5
	Ann Greenhalgh of Chorley in Lanc'	20	– 5
	Ellen Bradshaw[115] of upholland in Lanc'	14	– 7
	Annas Liniare of Leverpoole in Lanc'	30	– 4
	Ellen Leed of Sawick[116] in Lancashire	26	– 5
	Jane Vexon of Houghton in Lanc	16	– 5
	Sarah Reed of Wrixham in Wales	20	– 5
	John M[ck]Gee of Scotland	15	– 5

---

[111] Kelsall(?).
[112] Robert Harrison, "son of a Beggar Woman," bapt. 17 Apr. 1692 at Croston, part of which parish was Bretherton.
[113] At Upholland, parish of Wigan : Mary, dau. of James Winstanley of Winstanley, bapt. 23 Dec. 1684. Mary, dau. of John Winstanley of Orrall, bapt. 11 Jan. 1690. John, s. of John Winstanly of Orrell, bapt. 1 May 1664.
[114] Samlesbury.
[115] Eline, dau. of John Bradshaw of Upholland, Senior, bapt. 16 July 1692 at Upholland.
[116] Salwick.

Margaret Griffith aged about Eleven years of Carnarvanshire
to serve 7 Yeares to M[r] Lancaster or Assignes

To M[r] Ralph Williamson	Age	yeares of Service
February } Ann Cuquith of prescot in Lancashire	22	– 4
1705 } Dorithy Davies of Denby in Wales	20	– 4

To M[r] Edward Tarleton

February 1705 (Ralph Banckes of Bold in Lancashire	14 – 7
{ Robert Evans and Ann his wife of Dodleston	
(Cheshire	4
March 6 1705/6 Georg Robinson of Astick in Yorkshire	13 – 6
6 Thom' Hill of Hollingworth in Lancash	16 – 7
21 W[m] Fallar of or near Chedel in Cheshir	17 – 5
23 Ralph Collier of Rochdale Cloathworker	25 – 4

To m' Tho: Dutton Narrgat'

March 23. Jane Platt of Sropenhall[117] in y[e]: County of Chestr	
1705/6 Singlewoman	18 – 7
ead die Martha Platt of y[e]: same place Single'	14 – 8
ead die James Platt of y[e]: same	12 – 9
April 6. 1706 Eleoner Holford of Croton in Cheshire	15 – 6

To m[r] Parr and Worthington

February } 1705 }

Ellen Sedden
Robert Benson
Mich[l] Hogg
Alex Orrell
Alice Steele
Alice Monding
Ann Chandler
Ellen Pierson   mem'd Sarah Mere
Mary Worrall

To M[r] Jn[o] Lancaster Ann Cooke of Wales aged about 18
yeares to serve 5 years.

February } To M[r] Ezekiel Parr	age	Time of Service years
1705 }		
Margaret Tongue of Manchester Spinster	19	– 5
Ellen Taylor of Mchester	19	– 5
Margtte Roberts of Merionetshire in Wales		5
Mary Thornton of Stanney in Cheshire	18	– 5
Prudence Smalwood of Malpus in Cheshire	20	– 5

To m' Tho: Williamson Merch[t]

March 26. 1706 Roger y[e] son of James Rigby of Heay in y[e]	
County of Lan'	11 – 8

[117] Plainly so in the original, but probably meant for Gropenhall.

March 26. 1706 To m^r: J^{no} Smalwood w': goes in y^e: J^{no} & ⎫
        Thomas) Wm Sharples[118] of Lealand in y^e: ⎬ 25 – 4
        County of Lancst Taylor ⎭

March 28. 1706 to m' Thom' Williamson
        Jonath' Delnow of Trafford in ye County of
        Chester pd   11 – 9

To m' Wm Everard
April 1^t 1706   Tho : Edge Son of Thom' : Edge of Milton Green
        in Cheshire pd   16 – 7

To m' Georg Battersly
April 12. 1706 Thom' : Brown of Mansfield in Nottingham-
        shire pd   15 – 7

To Capt Tarlet
April 15. 1706 Wm Lucas of Worseley in Eccls Parish in Ches-
        hire pd   19 : 4

To m' J^{no} Tunstall
April 18. 1706 Elizabeth Brining of Samsbery[119] in Lancashir 17 : 7
        Ann Harrison of Frodsham in Cheshire   18 : 7
        Wm Robinson of Wimerley[120] near Garston in
        Lacast   17 : 7
Apr'. 22. 1706 Richd Glouer   22 : 7
April 27. 1706 Mary Greaues of Halton in Cheshr Singlewoman 27 : 7
        Ann Whalley of Broughton in Lanc.   23 : 7
        Ann Kerchin of Scazbricke   26 : 7
    29. 1706 Ellen Fisher of Wrightlington   18 : 7

To Thomas Johnson Esqr : for ye use of ye Own^{rs}
June 21. 1706   of Richard Rogerson of Bunbery in Cheshire age Time
         pd   18   07

To m' Thom' Woodward
July 20th 1706 Ambrose Wynne of Mould in Flintshire   20 : 06

To m' : Gilbert Lievsay, p Capt Edward Rochdale
July 16   Thomas Jackson of Millam in y^e : County of Cum-
        berland Taylo'   18 : 04
Augt 3   Jane Lievsay of Samsbury[121] in y^e : County of
        Lancs^t Spins^t 20 : 05
    6.   Mary Taylor of Burnley in y^e : County of Lancs^r
        Spinst^r 17 : 05
    8.   Jane Williams of Denbigh in Wales   29 : 04

---

[118] At Leyland : William, s. of Roger Sharples of Leyland, bapt. 30 Nov. 1679. Roger Sharples and Anne Fareclough, both of Leyland, m. 18 Dec. 1677.
[119] Samlesbury.
[120] Wimbersley.
[121] Samlesbury.

7b.	9.	Elizabeth Willson of Ellell in y[e] County of Lancastr Spinst[r]	19 : 05
	16.	Rowland Evans of Lang Gelly[122] in Wales Age	12 : 07
8b.	3.	Ellis Davies of Reabban[123] near Wrexham in Wales	20 : 04
	8.	Eliz : Eccleston of Polton in Lancashire Spinst[r]	20 : 05
	14 :	Joannah Meredith of Much Wootton in Shropshire Singlewom'	22 : 05
	15.	J[no] Jordan of Sheffield in Yorkshire pd	15 : 08

To Cap[t] J[no] Wright for Virgin', Maryland, or any of
y[e] Charybbee Islands

	age	yeares
December 9 1706 Tho : English of Cresleton[124] in Cheshire	14	7

To m' : Andrew Moore or Manchs[t] Jan'. 25. 1706

	Age	Yeares
William Dale son of James Dale Late of Manches[t] Taylor	15	5
Tho : Morley Son of W[m] Morley late of Walden in Kent Brickmk[r]	16 – 5	
John Heyes Son of George Heyes of Manchester Schoole Mast[r] January y[e] 28th 1706 p[d]	15 – 5	

To M[r] Thomas Hughs of Liverpoole Jan[r] 28 1706

Roger Ellors of Rochdale a father and Motherless Child	14 – 7	
John Walker of Cockerham, a Fatherless Childe	12 – 9	
John Grene of [ ]	14 – 7	
Margaret Jones of Holiwell in Flintshire	16 – 7	

These 4 Serv[t] were bound p Ad[m] J[no] Clievelands order to m' : Thomas Hughes and the charg[s]. (being Twenty shillings) place[d] to s[d] Ald[m]. Clievelands Acc[t] :

21. xb :	Margtte Smith of Lowton	16 – 5
21 ib :	Mary Brown of Langton	19 – 5

To m' : Thomas Williamson Merch[t] Febr : 4 : 1706

Rebeccah Shaw[125] of Macclesfield in y[e] County of Chest[r]	20 – 5	
Aarron Thornley[126] of Macclesfield p'	15 – 6	

To m' Georg Tyrer Janu'. 4. 1706. Rob[t] Dixon of Ulfall[127] in Cumberland   16 – 7

Feb. 12. 1706 Thomas Wild of Polton Taylor	20 – 5	
12 : 1706 Gilbert Periew[l] Son of James Periew[l] of Lymme Cheshire	15 – 7	

[122] Llangwyllog.
[123] Ruabon.
[124] Christleton.
[125] At Macclesfield : Rebecca, dau. of Edward Shaw of Crooked yard, bapt. 11 Mar. 1671-2. Rebecca, dau. of Samuel Shaw of Macclesfield Forest, bapt. 7 May 1672.
[126] Aaron, son of John Thornley of Macclesfield, bapt. 6 May 1691.
[127] Ulpha.

To m' : J^{no} Molyneux Merch^t Edmund Atherton
of Bolton Smith   20 : 4

Feb. 21st 1706 Mr Andrew More of Manchester
Mary Williamson Daughter of Sam^{ll} Williamson
late of Manceser   15 – 6

Feb. 27. 1706

To m' Thomas Preem Kather' Robinson of
Wrexham Denbyshire   20 – 5
Martha Lloy^d of Wrexham   p^d 20 – 5

March 17. 1706/7 To m' : Anth^y Booth J^{no} Davies of Wrexham
in Denbyshire but to serve in a sloop or to
y^e : Charybbees   17 – 5
Wm Robinson Son of Tho : Robinson late of
Dunfreeze in Scotl'   18 – 5
Henry Wainwright Taylor Son of J^{no} Wainwright late of Rainhill p^d 18 – 4

March 21. 1706/7 to m Georg Duddell, Wm Leatherland of Sut-
ton Weaver   20 – 7

Alice Leech[128]

[128] This entry, with the first name crossed out, is at the extreme lower edge of the page, and is the final entry.

INDEX

Abraham, Richard 32
Acres, Ellen 19
Actin, Elizabeth 41
Adams, John 17
　　　　Richard 4
Addison, Elizabeth 26
Adrick, Mary 39
Alcock, Richard 9
Aldorson, James 38
Aldridg, Michael 34
Alicer, John 28
Allam, Mary 35
Allison, Sarah 26
Alvin, John 8
Amery, Thomas 44
Anderton, Mary 22
　　　　Richard 36
Andrew, John 20
Archdeacon, Katharine 41
Arthur, Gryffith 24
Ascome, Thomas 28
Ascroft, Henry 26
Ashley, Ann 27
Ashton, Edward 43
　　　　Elizabeth 12
　　　　John 38
Ashworth, John 28
Askie, John 35
Aspinwall, Henry 42
　　　　John 42
Astly, Melicent 35
Atherton, Edmund 48
　　　　Peter 5 18 22
Atkinson, Mary 20
Auger, Adam 28

Babington, Thomas 7
Baddoe, George 7
Baggeley, John 7
Bagshaw, Benjamin 23
Baker, John 15
Balie, John 30
Ball, Edmund 18
　　　　John 35
Bamster, John 41
Banks ⎰ Jane 14
Banckes ⎱ Ralph 45
Bantum, Margaret 16
Barber ⎰ Charles 16
Barbur ⎱ James 16
Barlor, Charity 6
Barlow, Elizabeth 7
　　　　Ellen 17
　　　　Richard 24
　　　　Thomas 23
Barnes, James 27
　　　　John 18
Barroms, John 31
Barton, James 11
　　　　William 23
Basnett, — Mr. 30 34
Bate, Ralph 37

Battersly, George 46
Beaver, John 19
Beck, William 16
Beckett, John 29
Beecham, John 10 11
Bell, Henry 6 11
　　　　Joseph 19
Beniford, William 35
Benn, William 22 29 35
Bennet, Jane 24
　　　　William 7
Benson, Robert 45
Berkett, Thomas 22
Berlow, Richard 20
Berrey, Richard 41
　　　　Samuel 43
Bevis, David 13
Birch, Anne 32
　　　　John 40
Birchenough, James 26
Bird, Andrew 32
　　　　John 6
Bishop, Margaret 19
Blackwell, Ayley 14
Blake, John 5
　　　　Margaret 5
Blandford, Alexander 28
Blundell ⎱ ── 41
Blundele ⎰ Bryan 3 6 21 29 39
Brundell ⎱ John 41
　　　　Margery 3
　　　　Richard 41
　　　　William 16
Blyth, Ann 6
Boardman, Andrew 12
　　　　Deborah 12
　　　　Francis 21
　　　　James 12
　　　　Mary 10
Bole, Peter 19
Bond, Henry 6
　　　　James 6
Bonns, John 41
Booth, Ann 42
　　　　Anthony 48
　　　　James 42
　　　　Mary 32
Boucker, Jeremiah 30
　　　　Mary 32
Boudler, James 6
Bouldler, James 11
Boulton, Jacob 9
Bow, John 43
Bower, Francis 11
　　　　Robert 11
Bowker, Abraham 32
　　　　John 32
Bowland, Ann 40
Bowling, Thomas 21
Boy, William 31
Brachall, Thurstan 35
Bradburd, John 43

Bradbury, Thomas 30
Bradshaw, Abigail 34
　　　　Ellen 44
　　　　John 44
　　　　William 17
Bramwale, Jo. 9
Brascoup, John 26
Brasfeild, George 11
Breerely, Samuel 31
Bretherton, John 18
Bricknell, John 43
Bridg, Hannah 41
　　　　Richard 10 22
　　　　Sarah 32
Briggs, Elizabeth 32
　　　　John 14
　　　　Joseph 29 38 39
　　　　William 32
Bright, John 7
Brindley, William 35
Brining, Elizabeth 46
Briscoe, Thomas 33
Brittin, John 34
Brobbin, Elizabeth 9
　　　　Henry 9
　　　　John 9
Brooke, Nicholas 25
Brookes, Elizabeth 44
Brosents, Joseph 15
Brosier, Joseph 7
Brown ⎰ Ann 42
Browe ⎰ Henry 6 10 11 21 31
Browne ⎱ 35 37 39
　　　　James 38 42
　　　　John 5 14
　　　　Margaret 29
　　　　Mary 47
　　　　Samuel 32
　　　　Thomas 46
Bruin, John 13 15
Brundell, see Blundell
Buckley, Ann 30
　　　　Edward 7
　　　　Jane 30
　　　　Robert 37 38
Bulcock, Thomas 27
　　　　William 27
Bumber, Edward 23
Burgesse, George 39
Burl, James 36
Burnett, Abigail 14
Burnsides, William 13
Burridg, Daniel 28
Bushell, William 10 11
Butler ⎰ Elizabeth 40
Buttler ⎱ Thomas 34
　　　　William 34
Butterfeild, Henry 26
Butterworth, Adam 12
　　　　James 12
　　　　Judith 13
　　　　Nicholas 31

Buttler, *see* Butler

Camell, Elizabeth 32
Care, Martha 17
   Mary 17
   Samuel 17
Carefoote, Ganther 34
Carneagee, John 10 11
Carpenter, Isaac 12
Carr, Augustine 5
Carters, Rundle 33
Cartwright, James 32
   John 24
Case, Mary 17
Catterall } Alice 12
Cattarall } Francis 12
Cave, Elizabeth 24
Celliam, Sarah 13
Chaddock, James 19
   Thomas 43
Chadwick } Alice 39
Chadwyck } Jane 36
Chalis, Robert 9
Challinor, Alexander 15
Chanceller, William 5
Chandler, Ann 45
Chantrell } William 3
Chantrele }
Charters, John 30 34 38 39
Cheetum, John 15
Chestain, Benedict 30
Child, Daniel 14
Cholmondeley, Margaret 44
Chorter, Thomas 35
Christian, Stephen 39
Clark } Andrew 35 36
Clarke } Edward 15
   James 19
   Jonathan 10 11
   Robert 9
Clayton } Mary 26
Claytn } Thomas 12
   William 4 20 25 29
Clements, Jane 40
Clew, Daniel 19
Clievelands, John 47
Cloud, Mary 9
Clough, Sarah 31
Clowd, Mary 14
Clows, Daniel 18
Coales, Margaret 27
Cocke, John 30
Cockett, Ralph 34
Cockshutte, John 41
   Lawrence 43
Collier, Ralph 45
Collins, William 14
Coloct, John 30
Colson, Thomas 21
Conley } Isabel 3
Conly } William 21
Connily, Thomas 24
Cook } Ann 45
Cooke } Edward 19
   Ellen 5
   Thomas 4
Coop } Charles 12
Coope } Elizabeth 12
   Lawrence 12
Cooper, Elizabeth 40
   Joyce 11 17
   Mary 42
Corrwinn, Margaret 24
Corry, James 14
Cotton, Elizabeth 29
Coulburne, Ann 8
Coverly, William 27
Cowlund, Richard 5
Cowly, Mary 9
Cragge, William 17
Crampton } Walter 13 15
Cramp } William 13
Crane, John 43
Crimes, Jonathan 25

Crompton, Alice 44
   Elizabeth 13
   William 13
Cronage, Jeremiah 29
Crosbie, Joseph 23
Crosfield, Anna 36
Croston, Ellen 42
Croswell, Hannah 40
Curran, David 22
Cuquith, Ann 45

Dagnell, Samuel 17
Dale, James 47
   William 47
Dalton, Richard 22
Dangerfeild, James 12
Dann, John 17
Darrel, Richard 7
Darter, William 9
Davis } Charles 5
Dauis } Dorothy 45
Davies } Elizabeth 32
   Ellis 47
   Henry 5
   John 7 10 11 23 48
   Jonas 6
   Jonathan 5
   Maudlin 4
   Peter 23
   Robert 20
   Ruth 15
   Thomas 7 33
   William 8 17 22 24 33
Daw, Thomas 29
Dawson, James 39
   Mary 19
Day, James 22
Deakin, Esther 39
Delnow, Jonathan 46
Dene, Elizabeth 43
   John 23
Dewhurst, Arthur 28
Dickin, Elizabeth 17
Dickinson, Margaret 40
   Thomas 41
   Timothy 37
   William 7 21
Diggles, Alice 23
Dinsdall, Richard 34
Dixon, Elizabeth 38
   Robert 47
Dobson, John 6 11
Dod, John 33
Douglass } James 14
Duglas } Thomas 31
Dounes, Lawrence 5
Drury, Eleanor 24
Ducker, John 6
Duckes, Thomas 9
Duddell, George 48
Duglas, *see* Douglass
Dumbile, Ann 15
Dunbalin, Thomas 6
   William 6
Dunkin, Patrick 24
Dutton, Thomas 45
Dyson, Abram 13

Earthead, John 36
Eaton, Sarah 29
Eccles, Ann 12
   James 4
Eccleston, Elizabeth 47
Eden, Gilbert 36 37
Edge, Thomas 46
   William 36
Edmunds } Grace 28
Edmund } John 8
   William 24
Edwards } Anne 32
Edward } Charles 31
   Dorothy 8
   Elizabeth 21
   Evan 25

Edwards } John 20
cont'd } Richard 7 9 20 23
   Robert 23
   William 31
Elleson, *see* Ellison
Ellis, Ann 28
   Charles 10 11
   Elizabeth 28
   Margaret 20
   Samuel 28
   Thomas 6
   William 8 11 20
Ellison } Henry 43
Elleson } Jane 43
   Thomas 38
Ellors, Roger 47
Elwood, Joseph 20 29
Emett, Robert 27
English, Thomas 47
   William 4
Ertome, William 7
Evans, Ann 15 45
   Edward 31
   Evan 30 33
   Henry 7
   Jane 7
   John 39
   Margaret 24 33
   Peter 23
   Richard 5
   Robert 45
   Rowland 47
   Thomas 4
   William 22
Everard } William 33 36 46
Evrard }
Ewes, Thomas 28
Exx, James 12

Fairclough } Ann 27
Fairlclough } Anne 46
Fareclough } Margery 27
Fortclough } William 27
Fallar, William 45
Fallowfield, Wharton 15
Fanco, Francis 30
Farar, *see* Farrar
Fareclough, *see* Fairclough
Farrar } Henry 3
Farar }
Farrel, Thomas 7
Farrington, Edward 24
Fartley, William 13
Faulkner, Mary 17
   Richard 23
Faurell, Daniel 37
Fauster, *see* Foster
Faux, *see* Fox
Fawsette, Thomas 43
Fenne, Thomas 32
Feshel, James 35
Fidians, Randle 33
Fin, *see* Finn
Finch, Robert 14
   Roger 41
   William 41
Finn } John 17
Fin } Philip 17
   Richard 17
Firth, Isaac 13
Fish, Mary 36 37
Fisher, Ellen 46
   John 14
Fitchgerrard, Edward 32
Fleetwood, Robert 20
Fletcher, Alexander 38
   Eleazer 24
   Jonie 31
   Mary 38 40
   Stephen 19
   William 25
Floyd, Mary 10
Fogg, Nath. 13
Fooles, John 37

Forber, Richard 37
Ford, Hester 12
Fortclough, see Fairclough
Foster) Elizabeth 44
Fauster) Ellen 31
  Jane 5
  John 6
Fox, Edward 19
  John 15
  Robert 9
  William 12
France, John 17
French) Elizabeth 8
Franch) Jane 23
  Lawrence 22
  Nicholas 14
Francis, Thomas 24
Frankland, John 32
Fuller, John 24
  Mary 24

Gage, John 31
Galliburn, Elizabeth 22
Galloway) Randle 3 4
Gallowai)
Gambell, James 12
Garnette, James 22
Gasway, John 12
Gath, John 33
Gaylen, Margaret 38
Gedlin, William 35
Gibbons, Sarah 17
Gibbs, Mary 12
Gibson, Joseph 33
  Matthias 43
  William 3
Gilburt, John 14
Gildart, Richard 40
Gill, James 27
Gillgrist, Lawrence 3
Glauford, Francis 17
Glave, John 28
Gleddale, Mary 18
Glover) Edward 19
Glouer) Richard 46
Goare, see Gore
Godwin, Michael 15
Goodwin, Ann 34
  Robert 33
Gordon, James 4 5 6
Gore) John 34 38
Goare) Mary 27
Gowen, Peter 32
Greaues, Mary 46
Green) ―― 3
Greene) Ann 5
Grene) John 34 47
  Thomas 35
Greenhalgh, Ann 44
  Elizabeth 21
  John 21
  Mary 44
Gregg, Joseph 35
Greggory, Sarah 26
Greue, see Green
Griffin) Edward 29
Gryffin) Henry 30
  John 4
Griffith) Elizabeth 8
Gryffeth) George 20
Gryffith) Hugh 4
  John 23 30
  Joseph 31
  Margaret 45
  Mary 7
  Maurice 25
  William 4 5 28
Grimshaw, Miles 10
Gryffeth, see Griffith
Gryffin, see Griffin
Gryffith, see Griffith
Gurdain, Samuel 32
Gurdon, William 34
Guy, Edward 23
  William 14

Haddam, ―― 3
Haddock, Richard 24
Haggarty, John 16
Hairclipe, Hannah 40
Halewood, Henry 18
Haliwale, Ralph 16
Hall, James 21 32
  Peter 40
  William 24
Hamer, James 35
Hamilton, Andrew 17
Hamlet, William 38
Hamson, Thomas 27
Hardgrace, Ann 35
Hardman, Edward 10
  Thomas 33
Harefoote, Mary 34
Harginson, Alexander 31
Harker, Thomas 25
Harlow, Alice 9
Harris, John 9
  Richard 26
Harrison, Ann 24 46
  Isaac 29
  John 5 10 11 25 33 37
  Peter 33
  Robert 44
Hart, Joseph 23
  Thomas 36
Hartless, Samuel 40
Hartly, Jonathan 19
Hartopp, John 16
Hatton, James 37
  Richard 36
Hawkshaw, George 13
  James 11
  Thomas 13 15
Hayes) George 47
Heyes) John 47
  Martin 3
  Sarah 12
  Thomas 29 34 43
  William 38
Hayward)
Heward) Ann 36
Hewood) Mary 42
Heywood) Roger 36
Heal, John 33
Heanes, Sarah 35
Heap, Mary 42
Heaton, Alice 12
  Edward 12
  Elizabeth 12
  Richard 12
  William 15
Hebbett, Margaret 31
Heendrey, Jonathan 43
Hemming, Samuel 10
Henry, John 29
Hertland, William 27
Heward, see Hayward
Hewitte, Hannah 42
Hewood, see Hayward
Heyes, see Hayes
Heywood, see Hayward
Hicks, Timothy 31
  William 31
Hide, Jane 10
Higham, Thomas 11
Hill, Thomas 45
Hilton, Andrew 42
  Richard 3
  Sarah 26
  William 42
Hoague, John 15
Hodgkins, William 15
Hodgkinson, John 33
  Thomas 22
Hodgson, Ellen 39
Hogg, Michael 45
Holden, Joshua 21
Holding, Elizabeth 15
Holford, Eleanor 45
Holgrave, John 18
Holland, Peter 14 25

Holmes) Ellen 42
Holme) Ezekiel 38
Holms) James 17 25
Hulme) John 42
  Marah 17
  Margaret 17
  Mary 17
  Richard 16
  Timothy 17
Holt, Ellen 20
  George 25
  William 5
Hoome, William 20
Horne, John 27
Horsbell, John 31
Horton, Jane 5
Hough, Thomas 42
Houghton, ― Alderman 16
  ― Mr. 25 29
  Edward 13
  Richard 41
Hougland, John 44
Houseman, James 26
  John 9 26
  Mary 26
Howard, Job 15
  John 35
  Mary 28
Howarth, see Howorth
Howell) Edward 8
Howel) Humphrey 10 11
Howorth) Esther 21
Howarth) James 21
  Thomas 23
Hoyl, William 36
Hubbart, William 23
Hudson, Thomas 28
  William 10
Hughes, Ann 28
  Edward 8
  Elizabeth 30 38
  Ellen 7 37
  Evans 23
  Griffith 33
  John 5 8 17 19 33 42
  Katharine 7 40
  Margaret 25 35
  Martha 23
  Michael 31
  Nathaniel 39 40
  Owen 8
  Peirce 23
  Richard 4 23
  Robert 8 9 33
  Thomas 8 23 25 39
    40 47
  William 8
Hughles, Hugh 19
Hulme, see Holmes
Humplrey) Anne 32
Humphrys) John 37
  Thomas 8
  William 25
Hunt, Elizabeth 15
  Margery 7
Hunter, Eliza 24
  John 38
Huntington, William 22
Hurd, Nicholas 19
Hussy, William 28

Ingham) Ellen 38
Ingam) Richard 38
Ireland, Christian 8
Isherwood, William 38

Jackim, Jacob 44
Jackson, Frances 27
  John 38
  Martha 16
  Peter 16
  Richard 38
  Robert 34
  Thomas 18 46
  William 29

Jakeman, Richard 38
Jameson, James 10
　　　　Thomas 36
Jaspers, Edward 36
Jayes, Robert 29
Jenkins ⎱ Joseph 7
Jinkin ⎰
Jinkins ⎱ Lewis 3 9 20
Jennison ⎱ Thomas 13 15
Jennyon ⎰
Jeoffrys, Constant 21
Jinkin, see Jenkins
Jinkins, see Jenkins
Johnson, — Mr. 41
　　　　Diana 16
　　　　Elizabeth 38
　　　　James 19 31 39
　　　　Jane 12
　　　　John 13 16 26 28
　　　　Sarah 39
　　　　Thomas 3 29 46
Jones, Alexander 26
　　　　Ann 4 7
　　　　David 33
　　　　Edward 4 6 8 9 22 31
　　　　Elizabeth 7 9
　　　　Evan 39
　　　　Hannah 6
　　　　Henry 9
　　　　Hester 31
　　　　Howell 31
　　　　Hugh 6 8
　　　　Isabel 42
　　　　Jeremiah 13
　　　　John 6 8 9 18 20 23 24
　　　　Lewis 23
　　　　Margaret 19 23 47
　　　　Mary 9 22 29 35
　　　　Maurice 23
　　　　Nehemiah 35 36
　　　　Owen 32
　　　　Peter 4 16
　　　　Richard 4 8 13 22 23
　　　　Robert 7 9
　　　　Rowland 5
　　　　Thomas 18 33
Jordan, John 47
Joyce, Robert 22
Justice, Henry 32

Kearfoote, Margaret 12
Kenardy, Hugh 28
Kennion, Daniel 28
Kerchin, Ann 46
Kershaw, James 21
　　　　Ralph 26
Kettle, Ralph 6 11
Key, John 29
Kilshaw, Martha 30
Kinder, William 21
King, Abraham 6
　　　　Ann 13
　　　　Elizabeth 6 16
　　　　Mary 26
Kirby ⎱ Stephen 26
Kirkby ⎰
Kirk, John 6
Kirkby, see Kirby
Kirkome, Ann 26
Kitchen ⎱ William 6 11
Kitchin ⎰
Knight, Jane 36
Knowles, Edmund 31

Lackey, Jane 20
Lamb, John 10 13
　　　　Margaret 24
Lancaster ⎱ John 36 37, 40 41
Lancast ⎰ 44 45
Lancst ⎰
Langdon, Katharine 42
Langley, Ralph 40
Latham ⎱ Richard 25 38
Lathom ⎰

Laurill, John 40
Lavinsley, Margaret 26
Lawrence, Mary 40
Lawson, Robert 16
　　　　William 9
Lea, see Lee
Leafield, Elizabeth 30
　　　　Robert 14
Lealand ⎱ Hugh 6
Leyland ⎰ John 3 12
　　　　William 34
Leasiter, Adam 26
　　　　John 24
Leatherland, William 48
Leavins, Thomas 38
Lee ⎱ Henry 39
Lea ⎰ Mary 19
　　　　Susan 32
Leech, Alice 48
Leed, Andrew 10
　　　　Ellen 44
　　　　Phebe 20
Leek, John 3
Leekenber, Thomas 41
Leighman, Paul 3
Leivsay ⎱ Gilbert 21 25 46
Lievsay ⎰ Jane 46
Lievsley ⎰ Jonathan 4 9 14 25
Livesey ⎰ 31
Lensey, Barbary 32
Leskonby, Thomas 31
Lethberrie, John 25
　　　　Thomas 25
Lewis, Elizabeth 40
　　　　Maudlin 19
　　　　Richard 14 33
　　　　Robert 14
　　　　William 4
Leyland, see Lealand
Lidnescey, Nathaniel 32
Lievsay, see Leivsay
Lievsley, see Leivsay
Linacre, Ann 39
Lindsay ⎱ John 22
Lindsey ⎰ Thomas 20
Lingard, Ann 40
　　　　Ruth 39
Liniare, Annas 44
Liphot, John 26
Lipscom, John 28
Livesey, see Leivsay
Living, John 40
Lloyd ⎱ Henry 40
Loyd ⎰ John 5 8 15 31
　　　　Margaret 23
　　　　Martha 12 48
　　　　Thomas 5 24
Lommas ⎱ Ann 21
Lomax ⎰ Anne 21
　　　　Elizabeth 21
　　　　Esther 21
　　　　Ewen, see Owen
　　　　Isabel 21
　　　　John 21
　　　　Owen 21
　　　　Richard 21
Lord, George 43
Low, — Mr. 41
　　　　Ann 21
　　　　Ellen 44
　　　　George 11
　　　　James 38
　　　　John 28 34
　　　　Samuel 7
Loyd, see Lloyd
Lucas, John 43
　　　　William 46
Ludloe, William 3
Lund, — Mr. 29
Lunt, Edward 21
　　　　Elizabeth 32
Lyon, Daniel 12
　　　　John 15

McCreky, Samuel 15
McDonell, John 28
McGee, John 44
Maddock, James 32
　　　　Katharine 25
　　　　William 31
Maires, see Mayeres
Man, Peter 40
Marchie, Martha 33
Markley, Elizabeth 6
Marland, Thomas 10 11
Marsden, Christopher 32
　　　　John 13 33 43
Marsh, Alexander 14
　　　　Elizabeth 29
Marshall, John 4 13 15 36
Martin, Andrew 14
Mason, John 5
　　　　William 5
Masson, Mary 30
Masterman, Ellen 22
Mather, Thursden 12
Matthew ⎱ John 30
Mathews ⎰ Peter 5
Matthews ⎰ Robert 7
　　　　Thomas 31
Maurice, Robert 26
Mayeres ⎱ Josiah 16 18
Maires ⎰
Meakin, Elizabeth 40
Medecine, John 35
Medgley, Samuel 34
Medley, John 30
Mendam, Charles 28
Mercer ⎱ John 37
Merce ⎰
Mere, Sarah 45
　　　　Thomas 42
Meredith, Joanna 42 47
Merton, Richard 5
Messenger, Richard 22
Midclare, Mary 26
Middleton, Robert 17
　　　　William 18
Miers, Esther 34
Milborn, Mary 19
Milener, John 16
Millard, John 43
Miller, Jane 40
Mills, Charles 25
　　　　John 19 25 31
　　　　Mary 32 41
　　　　Sarah 25
Molyneux, Diana 32
　　　　John 48
Monding, Alice 45
Monk ⎱ Janet 24
Munck ⎰ Joseph 24 25 27
Moody, John 19
Moon, Robert 30
Moore ⎱ Andrew 47 48
Moor ⎰ John 3
More ⎰ Mary 39
　　　　Thomas 8
　　　　William 9
Mooreton, see Moreton
Morden, James 16
More, see Moore
Moreton ⎱
Mooreton ⎰ Matthew 10 11 18
Moretown ⎰
Morgan, Jane 36
　　　　John 8 14 31
Morley, Thomas 47
　　　　William 47
Morris ⎱ Elizabeth 35
Morrice ⎰ Finlh 8
　　　　Hugh 23
　　　　John 23 24
　　　　Mary 32 36
　　　　Robert 33
　　　　Thomas 8
　　　　William 32
Mosley, Adam 44

Moss } Mary 12
Mosse } Thomas 29
Mosson, William 3
Most, Thomas 32
Mottersheade } Adam 16
Mottershed } Roger 16
Muddiford, William 27
Munck, see Monk
Murphey } Daniel 31
Murfey } Richard 20
Murrough, John 28

Naylor, Elizabeth 30 32
Needham, Sarah 44
Neild, John 10
Neilson, — Mr. 14
Newell } Matthew 12
Newall } Richard 10
Newton, John 13
    Martha 17
Nichols } Elizabeth 26
Nicholls } John 10
    Margaret 33
Nicholson, John 20
Noblett, Robert 14
Norman, Mary 9
Nutter, John 30
Nuttes, James 18
Nuttong, John 20

Oakes, Elizabeth 34
Oglebie, John 31
    Robert 34
Oldfiel } Adam 35
Ouldfield } Frances 26
Oldham, George 5
Oliver, William 44
Ollerhead, William 27
Oragehead, Mary 34
Orrell, Alexander 45
Ouldfield, see Oldfiel
Owen } Ann 24
Owens } Ellen 39
    Evan 18 29 30
    Henry 24
    Hugh 16
    John 6 8
    Jones 8
    Richard 6 10 30
    Robert 20
    Thomas 7 23 31
    William 16
Owery, Mary 33

Pamwitt, Elizabeth 32
Parifie, Gravill 22
Parke, Thomas 29
Parker, Alice 27
    Elizabeth 42
    John 21
    Thomas 42
Parkinson } Christopher 33
Perkinson } John 33
    Richard 23
    Robert 33
Parr, — Mr. 3
    Ezekiel 10 12 41 45
    Joseph 13 41
Parrey, Henry 23
    William 37
Part, William 30 34 40 41
Partington, Hugh 4
Patience, John 35
Patrick, Christopher 18
Patten, Hugh 44
Patterson } Herbert 13 15
Pattison } Rachel 33
    Thomas 13
Peak, Martha 13
Peares, see Pierce
Pearson } Ellen 45
Pierson } Richard 34
    Thomas 33
Peatiason, Ellen 12

Peling, George 36
    Richard 36
Pelkington, see Pilkington
Pelton, John 38
Penberry, John 14
Penkell, —— 38
    Peter 38
Pennant, John 16
Pennington, John 28
Penry, Ann 28
Percivall, John 44
Periesel, John 44
Perkinson, see Parkinson
Perry } Edward 11
Perrey } Henry 8
    Katharine 4
    Luke 36
    Thomas 8
Pers, see Pierce
Peters, William 36
Philips, William 37
Phithian, Thomas 25
Physick, Charles 27
    Ellen 27
    Thomas 27
    William 27
Pickering, Frances 26
    James 26
    Thomas 22
    William 26
Pierce } Hugh 23
Peares } John 33
Pers } William 33 34
Pierson, see Pearson
Pilkington } Agnes 17
Pelkington } John 17
    William 17
Pinkston, Sarah 15
Plaise, Margaret 20
Platt, James 45
    Jane 45
    Martha 45
    Mary 40
    Randle 37 41
Plowman, Jonathan 33
Plumb, William 29
Pollard, Ann 42
    William 27
Pollet } Robert 10
Pollett }
Pope, Thomas 30
Porter, — Mr. 6
    Anne 27
    Ellen 38
    John 16
    William 10 21
Posthous, John 16
Poston, John 39
Pound, Susanna 16
Powell, Henry 18
    Hugh 5
    Robert 20
    Thomas 6
Preem, Joseph 42
    Thomas 48
Preeson, see Preston
Preestley, Jonathan 14
Prescott } Henry 7
Prescot } John 6 12
Presscot } Thomas 12
Presson, see Preston
Prestidge } Roger 42
Prestidg } Thomas 40
Preston } Thomas 27 43
Preeson }
Presson } William 24
Preswicke, Roger 37
Price, John 10
    Robert 23
Prichard, see Pritchard
Prior } John 4
Prier } Katharine 39
    Peter 5
    Watkin 5
    William 9

Pritchard } Amy 28
Prichard } Thomas 4
Pritchett, Andrew 22
    John 6
Proctor, Henry 24
Proudlow, Pemberton 39
Pugh, Ann 35
Pye, James 15
    Mary 30

Quarryer, Charles 21

Radcliff } Jane 18 19
Ratleife } Thomas 26
Radley, Richard 32
Rallestr, Robert 10
Ramsbotten, John 14
Ratleife, see Radcliff
Rawson, Thomas 38
Redding, John 14
Reddish, Hugh 18
Reed, Sarah 44
Relict, William 17
Relshaw, Ralph 16
Renndle, Margaret 15
Reyburne, Joseph 6
Reynolds, George 25
    Nicholas 16 21
    Robert 25
Rhodes, John 20
Richards } John 20
Richard } Walter 34
Richardson, Ann 24
    Thomas 18
Richson, Jane 40
Ricketts, John 10 13
Ridgway, James 25
Rigby, James 45
    Roger 45
Riglie, Paul 13
Rimmer, John 22
Ripley, Henry 4
Ritchley, Katharine 16
Rithwell, Moses 36
Roadly, John 19
Roberts } Edward 5 8
Robert } Elizabeth 8
    Ellen 43
    Evan 24
    Gabriel 8
    Henry 30
    Hugh 4 23
    Humphry 5
    John 5 30
    Margaret 45
    Maurice 5
    Thomas 8 30
    William 5 23 43
Robertshaw, Thomas 27
Robinson, George 45
    Grace 41
    Jane 34
    Katharine 27 48
    Mary 38
    Thomas 28 48
    William 30 37 46 48
Rochdale, Edward 42 46
Rochett, Elizabeth 26
Rodan, Homer 14
Rogers, Elizabeth 31
Rogerson, Richard 46
Rollins, Elizabeth 12
Ronell, Richard 38
Roper, Thomas 17
Roson, Ellen 34
Rothell, John 15
Rothett, John 19
Row, Thomas 6
Rowland } Joan 4
Rowlands } John 30
    Richard 32
Royle } Benjamin 17
Royl } Henry 17
    Janet 38

Rudd, Abraham 14
John 14
Runn, Ou 20
Rushton, Ellen 20
Russel, William 4
Rustin, Richard 33
Rycroft, Joshua 34
William 9
Rylance, Jacob 21

Sadler, Samuel 29
Salsbury, Humphry 19
Mary 19
Sammell, Ann 23
Sanford, Samuel 38
Scarburrough, — Mr. 11
Schofield) Abraham 26
Scofield } Ellis 28
Scowfield) Henry 32 43
Isaac 21
James 21
Scotland, Lawrence 19
Scott, William 12 21
Scowfield, see Schofield
Seacome, James 25
Thomas 17
Seddon) Ellen 45
Sedden } George 26
Janet 26
Thomas 26
William 29
Sellors, Isabella 31
Shaftin, Rabm. 31
Sharp, Elizabeth 39
Sharpless) Anne 46
Sharples } Cuthbert 16
Margaret 26
Roger 4 46
William 46
Shaw, Edward 47
John 13 15
Rebecca 47
Richard 24
Samuel 47
Sheapheard, William 13
Shehy, Charles 8
Shellom, Peter 16
Shenock, William 27
Sherman, Agnes 28
Sherwood, Jacob 24
Sarah 26
Showland, Daniel 4
Sickley, Ann 13
Siddall) James 26
Syddale } Robert 32
Simner, see Sumner
Simons, Richard 32
Simpcock, Samuel 30
Simpson, — Mr. 14
Singleton, Ann 19
Richard 21
Sinkler, Alexander 11
Slater) Alice 34
Slator } Thomas 39
Smalley, Edward 35
Smallwood) James 34
Smalwood } John 36 39 43 46
Martha 22
Mary 16
Prudence 45
Samuel 22
Smalshaw) William 24
Snalshaw }
Smalwood, see Smallwood
Smethurst, Alice 26
James 26
John 26
William 42
Smith, Christopher 27
Ellen 27
Henry 20 32 42
John 19
Margaret 47
Mary 5

Smith) Nicholas 10
cont'd } Ralph 26
Samuel 27
William 4
Snailem) Anne 27
Snailum } Richard 27
Snalshaw, see Smalshaw
Somner, see Sumner
Southworth, Robert 28
Speakman, Mary 20
Spence, William 22
Spencer, Joshua 12
Spooner, John 30
Stabbs, Edward 21
Matthew 21
Stafford, William 30
Standish, Mary 17
Stanley, Elizabeth 44
Stannor, Richard 23
Stansel, Elizabeth 34
Stanthrop, Joseph 12
Statham, Mary 28
Staton, John 9
Stedman, John 6
Steed, Ann 37
Anne 38
Steel) Alice 37 45
Steele } Edward 6
Mary 9 22
Stewart) Anthony 25
Steward } Daniel 31
Stuart) James 28
Jane 42
John 4
Mary 40
Newman 15
Thomas 7
Stile) Joseph 4
Style } Richard 31
Stock, John 18
Stockton, Philip 39
Stol, John 7
Strachine, John 14
Streete, James 11
Strickland, William 40
Stringer, Thomas 19
Stuart, see Stewart
Style, see Stile
Sumner) Aaron 17
Simner } Adam 26
Somner) Elizabeth 26
Summers } Ellen 26
Thomas 26
Sutherland, James 29
John 29
Swindle, Jane 16 19
Syddale, see Siddall
Sylvester, Thomas 3

Tagg, Joseph 34
Tapley, Jonathan 41
Tarleton)
Tarlet } Edward 5 6 10 18 34
Tarletn) 42 45
Tarlton) William 37 43 46
Tatlocke, Edward 39
Taylor) Charles 11
Tayler } David 11
Ellen 45
Isaac 14
Jerome 28
John 14 15 43
Joshua 25
Margaret 39
Mary 19 23 35 46
Nathaniel 11
Roger 12
Thomas 11 41
William 11
Telson, Elkanah 5
Terpin, Mary 10 16
Terroy, John 27
Thelfell) John 6 11
Threlfell }

Thelwell, James 28
Thomas) Elizabeth 24 35
Thoms } Gaynold 6
Gryffith 6
John 4 5 6 7 8 9 10
20 24 29 30
Katharine 30
Ralph 16
Richard 19
Rowland 9 24
Stephen 22
William 13 25
Thompson, Elizabeth 31
James 18
John 14 17
Joshua 35
Lawrence 25
William 22 29
Thoms, see Thomas
Thorncroft) Edward 10 11
Thornicroft }
Thornley, Aaron 47
John 47
Thomas 32
Thornton, Mary 42 45
Thorp, John 22
Matthew 22
Threlfell, see Thelfell
Threlford, Elizabeth 28
Tickle, Jane 19
Peirce 19
Tildesley) James 37
Tildesly }
Tipping, Dorothy 39
Todd, Margaret 19
Tomlinson, Richard 23
Tongue, Margaret 45
Robert 6 11
Tonnard, John 4
Tool, Ann 37
Toppin, James 29
Topping, Hugh 33
Towning, James 33
Travers, John 22
Troughton, Isabel 9
Troughweare, Joseph 6 11
Tucker, James 18
Tue, Mary 7
Tunstall, John 46
Joshua 28
Turner, Henry 26
Isabel 27
Robert 27
Thomas 12 27
Twiddale, Robert 24
Tyler, Thomas 20
Tyrer) Alexander 36
Tyror } Christopher 28
Tyrr) George 37 47
John 16 36

Upton) Elizabeth 16
Vpton } James 16
John 16
Margaret 30
Thomas 11 16

Valentine, Elizabeth 15 37
Vandery, Francis 43
Vaughan) Elizabeth 34
Voughan } Hannah 7
Robert 10
Thomas 10
Vavasor, Ann 26
Vexon, Jane 44
Voughan, see Vaughan
Vpton, see Upton

Wainwright, Ann 41
Henry 48
John 29 48
Walbanck, Henry 31
Walker, Ann 28
Daniel 15

Walker { James 4
cont'd { John 10 11 18 24 47
Mary 28
Thomas 10 11 28
Waller, Ann 27
Wallington, Samuel 4
Walls, John 12 24
Walmesley } John 27 43
Walmsley }
Ward, Elizabeth 26
Robert 17
William 26
Waring, Agnes 17
Margaret 26
Nathaniel 24
Samuel 25
Warner, Robert 8
Warrington, Edward 24
Waters } Elizabeth 28
Water } William 26
Watkins, Amy 7
Ann 8
Watkinson, Elizabeth 40
Watson, Samuel 39
William 39
Webb, Edward 37
Richard 37
Webster, Charles 8
John 3
William 4 7 8 9
Welsly, Margaret 35
Wennington, Joseph 27
Wentworth, Michael 35
Werton, Richard 5
Whalley, Ann 46
Oliver 12
Thomas 43
Wharton, Anne 30
Elizabeth 20
Thomas 39
Whitaker { Ann 43
Whitacre { John 32
Mary 23
Robert 32
Thomas 7
White, John 4
Whitehead, Jane 27
John 35

Whitlisse, Ellen 40
Whittle, Alice 27
Ellen 26
Nicholas 27
Widdop { Paul 18
Widop { Thomas 28
Wild, Thomas 47
Wilding, Thomas 10 11
Wilkinson, Charles 12
Williams { Ann 21
William { Daniel 33
David 23 33
Edward 15
Elizabeth 14
Henry 29 30
Jane 46
Joan 7
John 9 13 15 19 23
27 28
Katharine 9 37
Margaret 8
Mary 9 30 40
Matthews 19
Richard 23
Robert 7
Samuel 14
Thomas 14 17 18
28 29
William 18 23
Williamson, Mary 48
Ralph 28 32 37 43
45
Samuel 31 48
Thomas 34 37 40
41 45 46 47
Willington, Jane 26
Wilson { Edward 12
Willson { Elizabeth 6 16 47
Henry 36
James 29 32
John 4 12 30
Martha 40
Peter 38
William 5
Windsor, William 19
Winstanley } Henry 13
Winstanly } James 44
Winstantly } John 13 14 44
Winstonle } Mary 44

Winstanley { Peter 14
cont'd { Thomas 14
Wisson, George 14
Witter, Joan 17
Wood, Dorothy 37
John 12 18
Mary 37
Oliver 12
Samuel 37
William 15
Woodier, Katharine 41
Woods, Caelia 15
Henry 15 17
James 43
John 25
Mary 37 38
Richard 9
Robert 27
Woodward, Augustine 30 35
Thomas 46
Woolfet, Edward 28
Elizabeth 28
William 28
Woolley, Mary 41
Worden, Richard 8
Worrall, Mary 45
Richard 19
Thomas 33
Worrs, George 3
Wright, Elizabeth 33 34 38
Jane 22
John 11 42 43 47
Richard 39
William 33
Wynn } Ambrose 46
Wynne } John 10 11
Yales, Hannah 35
Yates, James 8
Thomas 16
William 40
Yeoman, Elizabeth 44
Young, John 17

INCOMPLETE NAMES

Bertinsh[ ] Alice 40
Fothn[ ] Peter 8
Granth[ ] Jane 37

H[ ] Stephen 36
Periewl[ ] Gilbert 47
Periewl[ ] James 47

Ratt[ ] Robert 31
Su[ ] Abraham 36